LABOUR CONDITIONS
IN WESTERN EUROPE
1820 to 1935

LABOUR CONDITIONS IN WESTERN EUROPE

1820 to 1935

By

Jürgen Kuczynski

LONDON

LAWRENCE AND WISHART

PREFACE

THE first part of this book is a rather long theoretical introduction into the study of labour conditions in Western Europe. It purports to give a survey of the methods of measuring labour conditions.

The four following parts deal with actual labour conditions in England, Germany, and France since 1820. These chapters combined do not take more space than the theoretical introduction. And most of the things to which attention is called in the first part are neglected in the rest of the book, because the statistical material available does not permit their being taken into consideration.

And while the theoretical part tries to show that real wages are by no means the only and not always the decisive factor determining labour conditions, the study of actual labour conditions is based, as far as statistical evidence is offered, chiefly on wage data.

The author's excuse for the publication of this book in this form at this time is a twofold one. Firstly, he believes that the approval of his proposals as to the methods to be applied to the measurement of changes in labour conditions might lead to a more intensive and more extended study of the history of labour conditions during the last hundred years. This study has been sorely neglected, and the author, therefore, thought that this part of his study should be published now. Secondly, since there is at present not a single research organization engaged in studying the history of labour conditions, and since only such an organization could gather an adequate amount of statistical evidence as to the development of all the factors influencing labour conditions, the author wanted to publish at least some data on wages as one of the most important factors determining labour conditions. And since our knowledge as to the movement of many other factors, influencing labour conditions, is large enough to judge at least the trend of their movement, it was possible to indicate not only the change in wages but also the general movement of labour conditions in England, Germany, and France since about 1820.

October, 1936.

JÜRGEN KUCZYNSKI.

CONTENTS

vii

CHAPTER I

THE MEASUREMENT OF LABOUR CONDITIONS

INTRODUCTION

THERE are few economists and politicians in any country who have not at least touched in their speeches, or have written articles or pamphlets or books, on the development of labour conditions.

Some of them have given us deep and clear insight into the status of labour. Among them those whose statements make up the early English blue books, many of the contributors to the German *Jahresberichte der Gewerbe-Aufsichtsbeamten und Bergbehörden*, or, to choose the most recent example, the collaborators in the *Preliminary Report on Study of Regularization of Employment and Improvement of Labor Conditions in the Automobile Industry* made by the N.R.A. to the President of the United States.

Some have written classic descriptions of labour conditions at a certain time, in a particular industry or country. Like Engels and Marx, or, choosing a lesser example belonging to this century, like Upton Sinclair in his *Jungle*, they have blended all the material available into unique pictures of suffering mankind.

None of them, however, have worked out a system for observing changes of labour conditions. None of them have tried to stipulate for any one time the factors which should necessarily be taken into account if one wants to investigate labour conditions. Without such a system of devices only the most gifted economist may proceed, while the great mass of honest students of labour conditions must necessarily be led astray or be induced to give wrong weights and emphasis to the many individual factors which only in their right combination give us a true picture of labour conditions.

. . . .

1

Despite many obstacles raised by strong social forces our knowledge of labour conditions has increased manifoldly during the last century. An enormous mass of material becomes available each year. In general, very little use is made of it. Who, for instance, reads the most important reports of the health inspectors in the United States, England or Germany ?

Wage statistics are being studied more carefully. But who has ever investigated what wages mean for the working class : does a higher wage mean better labour conditions if health conditions in the factories deteriorate ? Does a higher wage mean better labour conditions if capital migrates to other countries and there employs cheaper labour ? Is a table of real wages sufficient to indicate changes in labour conditions or is it necessary to study other factors, and which are these factors ?

The task of working out a combination of measuring-rods for gauging changes in labour conditions probably far surpasses the capacity of individual students of labour conditions. In the following pages I want to do no more than give a few indications, set out a few of the problems which have to be faced, show up a few traps into which others and myself have fallen, and forestall some conclusions which seem as obvious as they are wrong.

.   .   .   .   .   .

All students of labour conditions agree to-day that a knowledge of wage changes is absolutely necessary in order to get a clear picture of the development of labour conditions. Furthermore, almost all of them agree to-day that wage statistics will, by themselves, give us a clear picture of labour conditions, but this latter consensus of opinion is not the outcome of repeated experiments leading, again and again, to the same result, does not derive from common knowledge passed down from generation to generation and tried anew by each succeeding generation of students of labour conditions : it is the unanimity of mere prejudice or of blind hypothesis.

The first problem to be dealt with therefore is : what importance may we attach to statistics of wages as a gauge for measuring labour conditions ?

I. WAGES

1. *THE COLLECTION AND STUDY OF LONG-RANGE WAGE STATISTICS—A SURVEY OF LITERATURE*

Wages have been paid to industrial workers for more than 150 years. But the collection of long-range wage statistics —covering a period of at least a couple of decades—did not start more than 50 years ago. About 100 years went by during which little attention was paid to the movement of wages. Many studies of changes of labour conditions were published, very significant material on changes of labour conditions was collected long before a more intensive statistical study of long-range changes of wages was undertaken.

The history of publications on the subject of long-range wage statistics begins at the end of the nineteenth century.

It is true, that already G. R. Porter in his *Progress of the Nation* at the end of 'thirties, put together several series of wage data pertaining to several trades and covering up to a third of a century—but Porter remained a solitary figure.

It is true, long-range wage data had been collected before. In part these compilations were made by employers' organizations such as the Chamber of Commerce of Reims at the end of the 'forties or the Chambers of Commerce organization of Wurtemberg at the end of the 'sixties. In part these compilations came to us through government publications such as the Tables of the Revenue, etc., of the United Kingdom, 1833 and 1834. But either the wage material was unreliable, or it did not cover year to year changes or it pertained only to one or two trades, and in no case was it ever analysed thoroughly.

England published the first thorough purely statistical study inspired by an interest in the actual course of wages, and attempting to awaken a more general interest in the subject. It was a government publication of "returns and statements relating to wages, which have appeared in Parliamentary papers for the last 50 years or more."*

About the same time, the United States Department of Labor began publishing a series of articles and books un-

* *Returns of Wages, published between 1830 and 1886.* London, 1887.

interrupted to this day, dealing with wage statistics, as wage statistics had and have nowhere else been dealt with.*
Carroll D. Wright, Commissioner of Labor, initiated a collection of wage data pertaining mainly to the United States and partly to Europe not only with the purpose of gathering together all the printed material existing, but of preserving also many unprinted records, reprieved from destruction by agents of the Labor Department or the State Department. These agents wrote to or visited many industrial establishments in order to get as many wage records as possible.

The U.S. Department of Labor was the first to gather continuous wage statistics going back over many decades, and to try to secure uninterrupted series of wage data for as many industries as possible.

England came next with the exemplary series of articles by A. L. Bowley and Henry G. Wood, in the *Journal of the Royal Statistical Society*, on wages in the United Kingdom during the nineteenth century. Bowley and Wood were the first to arrive at a dependable general index of wages for any country for a number of consecutive years.† They succeeded in gathering such a wealth of material that their collection of data for the nineteenth century has virtually not been added to during the more than thirty years which since then have elapsed.‡

More than ten years later Germany followed suit with two studies by R. Kuczynski, covering the years 1870 to 1909 for some of the more important industries in several European countries and the United States.§

More than twenty years passed, and then in France François Simiand published his book *Le Salaire*, in which

---

* The first Report of the Department, published in 1886, already contained most valuable information on wages, covering up to thirty consecutive years, but scattered among other statistics, and pertaining to only a few trades or establishments.

† The general wage data for England and the United States published in the September 1898 Bulletin of the U.S. Department of Labor, covered a few cities and trades in England, and only a few industries in the U.S.A.

‡ Wood also compiled a remarkable wage series for New South Wales, 1823 to 1898.

§ *Die Entwicklung der gewerblichen Löhne seit der Begründung des Deutschen Reichs*, 1909, and *Arbeitslohn und Arbeitszeit in Europa und Amerika*, 1870–1909, 1913.

he compiled the more important wage statistics for France.*

At the same time, the Institute for Social Sciences of the University of Stockholm published its survey of Wages, Cost of Living and National Income in Sweden, 1860–1930, containing very much Swedish material not published till then.

The work of Carroll D. Wright has been continued by his successors in the Department of Labor, and no country possesses a collection of wage statistics comparable to that of the U.S. Bureau of Labor Statistics. In addition, private statisticians and other government as well as private institutions have gathered, sifted and condensed into remarkable series, often covering half a century and more, by far the largest wage material available for any single country. To mention but a few : there is Wesley C. Mitchell's work on the years 1860–80, Abbot's, Burges' and Combs' on unskilled labour's wages during several decades, and the U.S. Department of Agriculture with Blodgett's study of wages of farm labour. Of course, an enormous amount of wage material is still hidden in the books of many an industrial establishment, and many new figures could be added to the collection of wage data available to-day in the United States by working through this material ; yet the picture of the movement of money wages in general which the data published up to now present for the United States would not be materially changed. On the other hand, the tendency to get at first a view of the general trend of wages has hitherto led to an astounding neglect of the study of particular features of the wage movement. No general study has been made of the comparative movement of wages of skilled and unskilled workers, of female and male workers, of wages in exporting and other industries, etc., for any considerable period of time and for consecutive years. Although quite a number of non-official institutions exist which investigate the trend of general business conditions, no such institution is to be found in the United States for studying the trend of labour conditions.

English statistics seem to have made one supreme effort

* The French Government study, *Salaires et coût de l'existence, Statistique Générale de la France*, Paris, 1911, contains excellent data on long-range changes of cost of living, but the few long-range wage data given, covering every tenth year since 1810 and every fifth since 1850, are of little value.

in presenting to the world the admirable collection of data contained in the articles of Bowley and Wood. Since then, nobody has tried to continue and enlarge the work done by those pioneer statisticians. No new data have been found, and the tables presented have not been analysed beyond the explanatory text in the articles of Bowley and Wood. The Ministry of Labour computes an index of current wage rates and corrects this index from time to time so as to include a little more, and by recalculation, improve the former data to the extent of half a per cent or less. But the study of the history of wages in England is dead.

In Germany nobody has collected wage data of the past or analysed the trend of wages for a larger number of industries or years—except for some rather haphazard and isolated wage data collections in Wurtemberg during the second half of the nineteenth century. In the beginning of the twentieth century, the trade unions began to collect current wage data for their specific trades, some of them covering a great number of workers, but not going far back. Before the publication of the two books by R. Kuczynski it was impossible to get even a faint picture of the trend of wages for a number of industries combined. Even R. Kuczynski restricted his studies to the building, printing, metal machinery, woodworking, and stone-working industries, adding some figures published by the government for the mining and transport industries. For the industries mentioned he collected by far the most detailed survey of wage data existing for any industry in any country for the years 1870 to 1909. Since then no one has done any appreciable amount of statistical work on wages in Germany during the nineteenth century, and up to 1914. As in England, the historical study of wages is dead in Germany.

In France, the level of the study of industrial wages is worse still. No other country has had so many and such extensive government wage surveys as had France during the nineteenth century. But the historical study of wage data is unknown in France, and even Simiand was satisfied with the mere bringing together of the official government and of some private data. He has not made statistical use of even a considerable fraction of the printed material available for the purpose of showing the trend of wages, and the form in which he has presented the material compiled is so inadequate that one can safely say that not as much as one book exists in France which gives even a somewhat blurred picture of the trend of average wages during the nineteenth century.*

The Swedish study mentioned has not yet been completed, but even so far it gives much more material on the development of wages in Sweden since 1860 than has been accessible up to now.

No other country (with the exception of absolutely spurious wage data for India) has published an amount of wage data sufficient to enable us to judge the trend of wages for even a fifth of the nineteenth century. Of course no country other than the United States has made any steps in the direction of analysing special aspects in the trend of wages. And even the United States has done but very poor work in this direction.

2. *WHAT WAGE DATA SHOULD BE COLLECTED?*

Although the collections of wage data existing are comparatively small, even in England and the United States, yet much has been written about the procedure of collection and the questions which should guide it. A student wanting to start a compilation of wage data and seeking information as to methods of collection and calculation need only turn to the various articles by A. L. Bowley or to F. Eulenburg's book, *Zur Frage der Lohnermittlung*. They will tell him rather exhaustively how to gather the material, how to arrange it, and call his attention to many pitfalls to be avoided in order to arrive at a general average figure showing the trend of wages.

(a.) *Hourly and Weekly Wages.—Time and Piece Rates*

We must distinguish between hourly wages and full-time weekly wages. Hourly wages increase more than weekly wages because, in the course of decades, the hours of work per week have the tendency to decrease, and an index of

* Mention should be made here of the work of the Vicomte d'Avenel *Histoire économique de la propriété*, 1200–1800, and of Rogers' *History of Agriculture and Prices in England*. They give many wage data and are an invaluable collection as far as former centuries are concerned, but they do not refer to the course of wages since the industrial revolution,

hourly wages tends to exaggerate the increase of the wage income per worker.*

Full-time weekly wages are either the result of hourly wages or of piece wages. If the hourly wage remains the same the full-time weekly wage varies with the number of hours worked per full-time week. If the piece rate remains the same, the full-time weekly wage may change even if the number of hours per week is constant.

If piece rates and hours per week remain the same the full-time weekly wage will be, above all, affected by the speed of the work. Workers working at piece rates usually earn more than workers paid by the hour. But their working pace is usually much higher. Their working pace also changes more than that of workers on time rates. It varies with the amount of work to be done : if much work is to be done they are speeded up far above their usual rate of speed. Therefore their earnings differ from week to week, and occasionally, the difference is considerable.

Wages of piece workers must therefore be used with caution, and while it may be sufficient under certain conditions to compare, for example, the full-time weekly wage of time workers for the first week in June of different years, it is not possible to compare in the same way the wages of piece workers, because in one year the week chosen may have been a rush week and in the other year a slack week.

Although the weekly wages of piece-rate workers are usually somewhat higher than those of time-rate workers, nobody knows—or has ever investigated—whether this difference has a tendency to widen or to narrow. Nobody has ever investigated, for a sufficient number of years, what the difference actually is. Nobody has ever investigated how much the percentage of piece or time workers changes. For no country do we have any knowledge on the subject except for sections of one or another industry for one or two, or even a few years more, which, however, are neither consecutive nor comparable as to general economic conditions.

---

* These and the following remarks only refer to the collection and analysis of wage data after the industrial revolution. Hours of work in England, for example, were longer in the beginning of the nineteenth century than in some decades of the eighteenth century.

(b.) Rates and Actual Wages

We must distinguish between weekly wage rates and weekly full-time wages, because the actual wage paid generally differs from the wage rate ; it is either higher or lower.

R. Kuczynski says in the introduction to his book on wages and working-time in Europe and the United States : trade union wage rates are to actual full-time wages as the temperature measured in the shade is to the average temperature ; in the sun the temperature is higher, of course, and in places where the sun never shines the temperature is lower. Yet science has chosen as standard the temperature as measured in the shade. Therefore he feels justified in presenting in his book not only data on actual full-time wages, but also data on trade union wage rates.

Of course, nobody could be blind to the importance of this, the greatest collection of trade union rates ever collected which we find in the book of Kuczynski for the years 1870 to 1909. But surely Kuczynski is wrong in assuming that wage rates as agreed upon between employers and trade unions have the same meaning in 1880 and in 1905. Already Bowley had pointed out that wage rates have the tendency to develop from maximum rates into minimum rates. At first, trade unions are quite strong in perhaps a few establishments, but cannot enforce trade union rates in a whole city ; later on, with increasing membership, they succeed in having wage rates accepted for larger and larger territories until, at last, wage rates are agreed upon for the whole industry of a country.

But even the advice of Bowley will not help the new collector of wage data. Nobody has ever published data for a consecutive number of years showing in what way and by how much actual full-time wages differ from wage rates. Not even Bowley for England, or R. Kuczynski for Germany, or Brissenden, Douglas or Lubin for the United States, could tell us how far apart were wage rates and actual full-time weekly wages in the eighties or in the nineties of the last century, or how much they differed in the first or the third decade of the present century.

It is even doubtful whether they could tell us if the margin between wage rates and actual full-time wages has positively narrowed, or if there was merely a tendency to do so. In England, the power of trade unions to enforce rates is barely greater to-day than it was in the years preceding the War. Crises and depressions have compelled many a worker to work at less than the official wage rate rather than be thrown out of his job. Quite a number of key workers are being paid more than the agreed rate. But the number of key workers tends to decrease. The percentage of salaried workers has increased considerably, and the strength of the trade unions among the salaried workers is not considerable. Nobody could do more than venture a pure guess as to the development of the difference between wage rates and wages actually paid per full-time week during the last quarter of a century in England. My own guess would be that the spread between wage rates or salary rates, and wages or salaries actually paid has not decreased during that time, that the tendency of wage rates to change from maximum rates into minimum rates has been counterbalanced by other tendencies.

It would be even more difficult to answer the same question for the United States. There we find a very important factor counterbalancing the above-mentioned tendency of wage rates : if trade unions become very strong in one part of the country and succeed more and more in enforcing their wage rates, the industry migrates to another part of the country where trade unions are weak and wages are low—compare, for example, the development of wage rates and wages and the changes in localization in the textile industry during the twenties of this century.

It is indicative of the low level of our knowledge of wages that, for no country do we know anything about the trend of wage rates as compared with full-time weekly wages during the last half century, nor do we know very much about the number and the actual influence of the various factors which counterbalance the tendency of wage rates to become minimum rates after having been maximum rates.

(c.) *The Time Factor*

We must distinguish between weekly full-time wages and wages actually earned per week. The actual weekly earnings (of time workers) are determined by the actual time, the actual number of hours worked during the week. This number of hours may be increased above the normal rate by overtime work, or it may be decreased by short-time work. Overtime work is sometimes paid at a higher rate per hour, and sometimes not. Short-time work is paid according to the shorter number of hours worked. In some cases salaried workers receive the same wage per month whether they work overtime or short-time.

Has overtime increased during the last decades or not ? Has short-time increased or not ? No one knows, for only very few countries have collected data on short-time, fewer still have collected general data on overtime (I know only of Czechoslovakia), and none of these have collected data for more than a few years.

It is, therefore, impossible to take into account, for any country, the amount of time actually worked if one wants to construct an index of wages during the nineteenth or twentieth century. For some countries one can compute the average normal length of the working week, for some countries one may guess at the amount of short-time, but no actual data are available for any of them.

As to the average yearly wage, it is quite different from a yearly average of weekly wages actually paid. The average yearly wage takes into account unemployment, in addition to short-time. First to compute a wage series taking into account unemployment was, as far as I can find, Wood* in the beginning of this century. Nobody followed his innovation during the next quarter of a century ; it was simply forgotten, and even to-day only very few statisticians take into account unemployment and short-time when they study the development of wages.†

Nobody has ever taken into account the losses of wages through illness. Nobody has ever taken into account the losses of wages through accidents and strikes. The data are

---

* H. Losch, *Die Arbeitslöhne in Württemberg, Württembergische Jahrbücher*, 1897, already demanded the computation of yearly average wages in order to be able to take into account unemployment, but he had no data on unemployment and therefore was not in the position to work on the Wurtembergian wages as Wood did on those for England.

† So far I found among long-range wage statisticians only J. Kuczynski first in his wage studies for Germany (and later for other countries also) in the *Finanzpolitische Korrespondenz*, 1929, and Paul H. Douglas, *Real Wages in the United States, 1890–1926*, 1930.

scattered and not easily put into shape—but this should not be sufficient excuse to prevent several generations of statisticians from putting a little more reality into their statistics. But aside from using accident and sickness and strike figures for computing average wage statistics—nobody even knows whether industrial accidents have increased during the last fifty years or not, whether health conditions have improved among workers or not, whether the loss of working time through illness or strikes has increased or not.

R. Kuczynski* and Ehrenberg† have published some statistics of life wages, to investigate how much certain workers earned during the greater part of their working life. Life wages are, of course, the ideal wages for measuring changes in the earning capacity of the worker. They take into account the increasing earning capacity due to the acquisition of greater skill and (or) the promotion to better positions within an industrial establishment. They take equally into account the decreasing earning capacity due to failing strength, failing health, etc. They take into account short-time, loss of employment, sickness and accidents, etc.

But if we look over the scanty figures available for life wages we find that they refer only to workers working during the whole time under review in one and the same establishment. They refer often to workers who have succeeded in improving their position far beyond the average or who, because of their close affiliation with the same establishment, were comparatively seldom out of work. These life wages show, therefore, a tendency to increase much more—or to decrease much less—than average wages. The material at present available for life wages is meagre, and those who would like to use it would have to be cautioned not to draw any general conclusions from it. They may ask why most of the data do not go further than pre-War times ; the answer is that the interest in long-range wage statistics has become even smaller than it was twenty-five years ago.

(d.) Neglected Deductions

Quite often workers get a wage which, at first sight, may seem to be higher than expected ; but at closer scrutiny it

---

* *Zeitschrift für die gesamte Staatswissenschaft.* Jahrgang, 1906.
† *Thünen-Archiv,* 2 und 3. Jahrgang.

shrinks by a fifth, a fourth and even a third of its original size owing to deductions of all kinds.

Such deductions are made, for instance, for taxes.* The changing burden of indirect taxation is taken into account if we compute real wages because prices change with indirect taxes. But direct taxes, in as far as they are paid by the worker, are not reflected in price changes. Now, in most countries direct taxation of the worker has gained in importance, and it is, therefore, necessary to make corresponding deductions from the workers' wages. But here again : the material available for estimating the percentage of wages absorbed by direct taxes is very scanty. There are practically no data for a consecutive number of years in any country which would enable the statistician to compute an index of the tax burden for the years preceding the War, or for the nineteenth century. And even for post-War years, only a few scattered data exist, the best being those for Germany.

Our knowledge is almost as meagre when we come to the payment of state insurance dues. These payments are mostly deducted from the weekly wage before the worker gets his pay envelope. And we know even less about the percentage of lost wages which the worker can recuperate through unemployment or sickness or similar benefits.

The only wage statistics for a consecutive number of years which take into account changes in tax and social insurance payments on the one hand, and changes in unemployment benefits on the other, are, as far as I know, my own statistics concerning England and Germany.† But though it is true that almost nobody has done more than mention the influence of these factors upon the actual wage received by the worker, it is at least a recognized fact that they do have some influence.

Another factor, however, making for a decrease of the wage actually in hand for providing a living has not even

---

* In case the tax is deducted by the employer (as in Germany) it must necessarily be deducted also from the wage used for compiling a wage series. In case the tax is paid by the worker after receiving the wage one can also add the tax to the expense account and thus include tax changes in changes of the cost of living.

† Cf., for example, *Die Entwicklung der Lage der Arbeiterschaft in Europa und Amerika*, 1870-1933.

been mentioned in literature : trade union dues. If they are at all thought of they are put down as one of many possible but by no means necessary items on the list of workers' expenses, such as a newspaper or a fountain-pen. In fact, they are by no means an item of expense which the worker may undertake or not, but they must be regarded simply as a deduction like taxes and unemployment insurance payments. Why should this be so ?

It is a recognized fact among all economists that money wages have increased because of workers organizing themselves into trade unions. Bowley's observation that trade union wage rates have the tendency to change from maximum rates into minimum rates means just that. Thus part of the increase of money wages—or their maintenance or their comparatively smaller decrease—is undoubtedly due to trade union activity. Now, one should not, on the one hand, compute an increase of wages, and on the other hand, not take into account the workers' expenses to get this increase —just as one should not, on the one hand, list the things a worker has bought and, on the other hand, neglect to set down the money he has paid for them. It is, therefore, necessary to deduct from the wages the average expenditure of the working class for trade union activity, an item which undoubtedly has increased very much during the last half century. And the same holds true, of course, of money collections for strike purposes.

(e.) Pitfalls of Averages

The smallest unit to which wage statistics can refer is one single person. Wage statistics pertaining to one person are of interest only as a sort of statistical wage biography. A biography from which one can of course not generalize, the story of an isolated part of humanity about whose relations to the whole of society one does not know anything. A single miner's wage tells us almost as little about the wages of all miners as about the general average of wages in all industry.

A somewhat larger unit is represented by the family, but the wage history of a miner's family is, as far as general conclusions are concerned, almost as barren as that of a single miner.

That does not mean that the investigation of wages of an individual worker or one individual family cannot be very useful. If one knows, for example, that the earning capacity of miners increases considerably during the first five years of their work, remains stable for the next twenty years, and then decreases quickly, this can be illustrated by the example of the life earnings of a miner week by week or year by year.

The smallest unit, useful under certain circumstances for drawing conclusions as to the trend of wages, is a prominent plant. Wages paid in the chief factory of the Imperial Chemical Company, the I.G. Farbentrust or the Du Pont Company can perhaps be called indicative of wages in the chemical industry in England, Germany or the United States. However, one may not call the results of such a wage study conclusive evidence.

Big industrial establishments may, for example, be well unionized and may therefore show a smaller wage decrease during a crisis and depression than the whole of the industry. Big industrial establishments may, for example, be not unionized at all, and may pay during prosperity a wage considerably above the average for the industry as a whole, but may decrease wages during the crisis more than the average. Big industrial establishments may, because of more thorough mechanization of the production process, employ more women than the average of the industry as a whole, and since women are paid less than men they may pay an average wage to their employees considerably below that for the industry as a whole. Big industrial establishments may just for the same reason, because of more thorough mechanization of the production process, speed up production to such a degree that the percentage of women employed has to be decreased and therefore they may pay an average wage above the average for the industry as a whole. Big industrial establishments may be much better able to weather a crisis than the average establishment, and therefore may be able to keep, though work is slack, a great percentage of their key workers on the pay-roll ; the dismissal of the great mass of workers and the keeping of key workers could lead to an increase of the average wage paid, and thus, while the industry as a whole would show perhaps a considerable decrease of wages, the big establishments would show even an increase of wages during the crisis.

All these examples show that wage averages for big establishments may be less indicative of the trend of wages than the average for many smaller ones, and that comparative bigness of the sample does not, by itself, make it under all, or even under most, circumstances, a better sample.

In addition, the last of the examples given shows up one of the pitfalls of averages. The average wage in a big establishment may increase during a crisis because of a comparative increase of the number of key workers, even if the wages of each individual worker decrease. Let us assume that in a big factory 1,000 workers are employed of whom 200 workers are key workers receiving each a wage of 50s. per week while 800 workers receive a wage of 20s. per week ; the average wage for the factory as a whole would be 200 times 50s. plus 800 times 20s. divided by 1,000, or 26s. per worker. During the following crisis the 200 key workers are kept on the pay-roll while 600 of the remaining workers are dismissed. Wages are slashed by 20 per cent for all workers, and therefore the factory would employ 200 workers at 40s. per week, and 200 workers at 16s. per week. The average wage per worker would be 28s. Thus while each worker gets 20 per cent less per week the average for all workers would have increased during the crisis from 26s. to 28s.

A most important conclusion may be drawn from this example : average wages refer always to a group of people, and the changes in average wages are not necessarily indicative of the changes of wages of the individuals belonging to this group. It is possible that the wage of each individual worker belonging to a certain group of workers decreases, but that the average wage of the group as a whole increases.

This holds true not only for an industrial establishment or for a single industry, but also for industry as a whole, for all the workers working in one country, and for all the workers working within one industrial society.

If we take, for example, the development of wages in England during the nineteenth century, part of the increase of the average money wage in manufacturing industry as a whole is undoubtedly due to the fact that textile workers are paid less than iron and steel workers, and that the number of iron and steel workers has increased much more than the number of textile workers.

One can enlarge the field of observation even more and include all the workers in England. Agricultural workers are paid on a much lower scale than industrial workers. Part of the increase of average money wages in England as a whole during the nineteenth century is due undoubtedly to the fact that the number of agricultural workers has decreased very much in relation to the number of industrial workers.

In each of these two examples the wage of each individual worker may have decreased and yet the average for all workers may have increased because of structural changes in the composition of the working population.

It is obvious that changes in the percentage of child workers and women can lead to similar discrepancies between the movement of the wage of the individual worker and the average wage of all workers.

On the one hand, it is therefore necessary in computing average wages to take into account changes in the structural composition of the number of workers, to make certain whether wage changes occur in relatively growing or declining industries, etc. (weighting the wage changes according to the number of workers affected) and whether wage changes occur in industries paying a wage above or below the average (weighting the wage changes according to the absolute wage level).*

On the other hand, it is not possible to draw conclusions with certainty from an index of average wages concerning the development of wages of all the individual workers belonging to this average.

.   .   .   .   .   .

One last pitfall of averages remains to be mentioned although it seems so obvious that only very inexperienced wage statisticians should be endangered by it. But as a matter of fact, as far as I can see, every wage statistician

---

* The formulas for computing wage indices taking into account these structural changes and the absolute level of wages have been worked out by A. L. Bowley, *Journal of the Royal Economic Society*, 1928.

including myself, has fallen into it when working on these specific problems.

In investigating the trend of wages over a longer period one of the most interesting problems is the question : have labour conditions deteriorated, do misery and destitution and wage slavery increase, or have labour conditions improved, is the status of labour a better one to-day than, let us say, 50 or 100 years ago?

None of those who are of the opinion that labour conditions have deteriorated in the course of time want to contend that every group of workers is worse off to-day than half a century ago. Those who believe that labour conditions have deteriorated are only thinking of the living conditions of the working class as a whole.

By working class as a whole they mean the English working class, the German working class, the French working class. The first to investigate these problems thoroughly was Marx. And he was right in confining his study to the workers in England because English capital employed almost exclusively English workers.

It was Lenin who, with the growing of capitalist society, enlarged the field of observation in his classic studies on imperialism. Most of these problems were touched upon already by Marx, but since they became of greatest importance as problems of capitalist society only after the sixties of the last century it was neither necessary nor possible to lay on these problems the emphasis which Lenin had to give them, and gave them.

Marx and Engels, and Lenin, analysed the problem of the labour aristocracy, and it was Lenin who clearly indicated the connection between the problem of the labour aristocracy and the capitalist exploitation of labour in the colonies.

But none of those who have made studies of labour conditions and who wanted to judge, for example, from the trend of wages in England the improvement or deterioration of labour conditions, took the hint contained in the theory expounded by Lenin and realized :

The Marxian theory, the Leninist theory contends that labour conditions deteriorate under capitalist economy and that to the accumulation of capital on one side corresponds the accumulation of misery on the other side. Therefore if one wanted to prove or disprove the Marxian-Leninist theory by wage statistics it would be necessary to compute the trend of average wages not only for key workers in the optical industry, not only for key workers in manufacturing industry as a whole, not only for all workers in manufacturing industry, not only for all workers working in England whether they be employed in manufacturing industry, agriculture or trade, but for all workers employed by English capital everywhere, in England or in Ireland or in India or in South Africa.

None of the experienced statisticians has tried to disprove the Marxian theory by showing that wages of especially skilled workers have permitted better and better living conditions during the last fifty years. But the best statisticians have made a very similar mistake in trying to prove or disprove Marxian theory by confining themselves to a study of labour conditions, for example, in England instead of taking into account—for the period after 1850—all the places where English capital employs workers in capitalist enterprises.

Trend analysis of labour conditions in general has always to start from the assumption that the factor which determines the size of the group to be investigated is the capital unit, and not the nationality of the worker.

"Polish labour conditions" does not mean conditions of labour of all Poles. One may be interested, of course, in the fate of Poles and compute an average wage for all Polish workers whether they work in a Lodz textile factory or in a Pennsylvanian mine or in an Argentine slaughter-house—but such an average would be without social significance just as the computation of the average height of all people born of parents of American nationality is without any racial significance.

Polish or English or German labour conditions means the condition of all workers working under Polish or English or German capital.

To-day, a juxtaposition of wages of English textile workers and profits of English textile capital would be a juxtaposition of the wages of workers working in England and English capital "working" in England and India and elsewhere. It is obvious that such a juxtaposition is illogical and without significance.

In computing an average wage for a particular country, England, for example, one certainly does very useful statistical work of a regional character and one certainly is justified in drawing conclusions from these computations as to the development of labour conditions in England. But it is quite wrong to draw from such an investigation any conclusions as to the development of the position of the worker in English economic society since English economic society extends far beyond the national boundaries of the British Isles.

(f.) Some Examples

Though on the average the difference between weekly wage rates and actual full-time weekly wages is not very considerable, at certain times or in certain establishments the margin may be quite large. As an example of a comparatively wide average margin we give wage rates of printers in Danzig and wages actually paid for a full-time week in a printing establishment in Danzig, always for one week in June in the years 1905 to 1910 (in marks) :

Year	Wage rates	Wages actually paid
1905	24.75	25.60
1906	24.75	25.75
1907	27.50	28.25
1908	27.50	28.30
1909	27.50	28.80
1910	27.50	28.90

The margin between wage rates and actual wages fluctuates between 3 and 5 per cent, and while wage rates remain the same between 1907 and 1910 actual full-time wages increase by several per cent.

Examples showing actual full-time weekly wages considerably below wage rates can be found easily in life but very rarely in print, and times of crisis and depression very often bring about a continuous decrease of actual wages while wage rates remain unchanged.

.   .   .   .   .   .

An interesting example showing the influence of short

time on wages actually earned, was given by E. C. Snow*
for the leather-tanning industry in England :

Year	Wage rates	Wages actually earned
1922	103	103
1924	100	100
1926	100	91
1929	100	97
1930	100	95
1932	95	85

Disregard of the official wage rate and short time may
bring down the index of actual wages in times of crisis by
10 per cent and more below the level of the wage rate index.

.   .   .   .   .   .

The enormous difference between wage rates and actual
wages obtained by taking into account also losses through
unemployment, taxes, and insurance payments on the one
side, and gains through unemployment insurance on the
other side may be seen from the following example :†

† Cf., *Finanzpolitische Korrespondenz*, Jahrgang XIV. Nr. 7/8,
Die Konjunktur für den Arbeiter, by Jürgen Kuczynski.

*Wage Rates and Wages Actually Earned per Week
in Germany, January, 1933*

Weekly Wage Rate	..	..	..	..	38.90	Mark
Average payment above wage rate		..	..	1.15	Mark
Losses through short time		..	..	2.40	Mark
Losses through unemployment		..	..	18.70	Mark
Taxes and insurance payments		..	..	2.65	Mark
Unemployment insurance benefits†		..	..	3.75	Mark
Actual weekly earnings ..	..	..	..	..	20.05	Mark

Actual weekly earnings are in this case only about half as
high as the average weekly wage rate.

* Discussion of the " *The Course of Wage Rates in the U.K., 1921–34*,"
by E. E. Ramsbottom, *Journal of the Royal Statistical Society*, 1935.
† Benefits, if received, are actually much higher, but many unemployed
had been deprived of their rights to receive benefits.

This example shows how utterly inadequate wage rates statistics may be, under certain circumstances, as a measuring-rod of the worker's actual weekly wages.

.   .   .   .   .   .

The great influence on the long-range movement of wages of the migration of workers from lower-paying agriculture to higher-paying industry, and from lower-paying industries, such as textiles, to higher-paying industries such as iron and steel, is shown by the following table. It is taken from an article of H. G. Wood* and gives an index of average wages in England for all workers and another index of wages as they would have moved if wage changes were the same as in the former index, but if the distribution of workers in agriculture and industry and in the individual industries had not changed during the whole course of time :

WAGES IN ENGLAND

(recomputed on the basis 1900 = 100)

| | Average Full-Time Wages | |
Year	Actual Average	Average Without Migration of Workers
1850	56	66
1855	65	75
1860	64	72
1865	71	78
1870	75	81
1875	86	92
1880	82	86
1885	84	86
1890	91	93
1895	91	90
1900	100	100

Fully one-third of the total increase of money wages between 1850 and 1900 as computed by Wood, is due to migration of workers from lower-paying to higher-paying industries—a migration caused by changes in the economic structure of society—and probably in part also by a decline of the percentage of children employed in industry.

This example shows how great an influence such structural changes may have. On the other hand, computations I made

* *Journal of the Royal Statistical Society*, 1909.

for Germany showed almost no difference at all. Other factors have, in this case, quite obviously counterbalanced the effects observed for England.

.   .   .   .   .   .

The foregoing discussions and perhaps more clearly the examples given show that an enormous field of investigation still lies before the wage statistician. Investigations which will at first lead him far away from wage data, such as an investigation of the rate of accidents, of short-time, of unemployment benefits, but which ultimately will help to bring us closer and closer to a true picture of the changes of wages actually available for the worker's household.

Although it may be doubtful whether an individual student would be able to do all this work for one country over a series of years, there can be no doubt that such work is necessary, that such studies should be undertaken.

The amount of money disposable for economic investigations by government agencies, scientific institutes, or research departments of commercial enterprises is by no means large, but it is more than enough to permit a thorough study of the course of wages since the industrial revolution in any of the more industrialized countries.

3.   REAL WAGES AND RELATIVE WAGES

Money wages have, of course, only a very limited value as a means of measuring labour conditions. They do not show whether in the course of time the worker can buy more or less. For a wage increase may be compensated by a greater price increase or a wage decrease by a greater price decrease, and vice versa.

Statisticians, therefore, have devised another measurement of wages : the real wage index. Real wages are nothing but money wages corrected according to price changes. The real wage index indicates the changing purchasing power of wages.

The measurement of price changes is, however, much more complex than it seems at first sight. It is not difficult, if the necessary price data are available, to compute an index of the prices of a certain kind of bread, let us say for the years 1920 to 1935. It is just as easy to compute such an index for the years 1820 to 1835, if the price data are available. It would be useless, however, to have the price data for one kind of bread for the years from 1820 to 1935 because to-day the worker does not buy the same kind of bread he ate 100 years ago. He may, e.g., have changed from bread containing more wheat to bread containing more rye, or vice versa. In order to compute an index of price changes of the bread the worker eats, one needs not only an index of the prices of a certain kind of bread ; one needs an index for several kinds of bread and one needs, just as much, information about the kind of bread the worker usually bought in 1820, 1850, 1880, 1910, etc. Even this is still insufficient. The worker not only changes the kind of bread he eats, but also the amount of bread. Undoubtedly the worker of seventy-five years ago spent a greater portion of his " food money " on bread and a smaller part on meat than to-day.

In order to compute an index of the cost of living it is therefore necessary to know : changes in prices, changes in quality, and changes in the relative amount of commodities bought.

But even this is by no means sufficient. Not only the relative amount of a given commodity the worker buys changes, the commodities themselves change. To-day, the worker no longer buys a number of goods he bought 100 years ago, and quite a number of the goods he buys to-day he did not buy in 1835. And often he is obliged to buy them under all circumstances ; tramway tickets, for instance, because of the increasing distance between the living and the working place.

In order to compute a cost-of-living index it is therefore necessary to construct a workers' budget including all the goods a worker buys ; to investigate how the prices of these goods have changed, and to modify the composition every ten or fifteen years according to the varying buying customs of the worker, by dropping or adding this or that commodity, and by increasing or decreasing the weights of the various items.

But not only custom determines the composition of the workers' budget, the level of wages itself brings about changes in the budget. And here we come to the greatest of all difficulties.

Let us first state the point at which we have arrived up to now. The statistician composes a workers' budget either on the basis of an existence minimum, or on the basis (as the official expression in the United States has it) of "health and decency," or on any other basis ; then he varies the composition of the budget in the course of time according to social or fashion changes. He can then calculate a composite index of the prices of the commodities collected on this basis (minimum of existence, etc.).

But is it right and justifiable to compute such a budget on the assumption that it is equally reasonable to measure the purchasing power of wages in times of prosperity and in times of crisis with one and the same measuring-rod, let us say by means of the health and decency budget?

The price movement in Germany during the years 1932 to 1934 will serve as illustration. The official index (though very deficient) may be said to be based on a health and decency budget. The average net wage per worker in 1932 amounted to little more than half of this budget. That means that the worker was not touched at all by quite a number of price changes which the cost-of-living index takes into account. Now, if one investigates the price changes a little more closely and computes, for example, an index of the changes of prices of a selection of foods such as the worker can really buy, and if one compares this index with food price changes according to the official index one finds, for 1933 and 1934, a price increase for workers four times as high as the one shown by the official index. The official index is, of course, computed correctly, but the weight the official index gives, for example, to the heavy increase in potato prices is very much smaller than the actual weight of potatoes in the workers' budget would call for ; for the official index includes many foods which the worker could perhaps buy in 1929 but can no longer buy in 1933, and which he replaces in part by much larger quantities of potatoes—potatoes being still much cheaper than the other commodities although their prices have, in comparison, gone up very much more.

We must conclude that it is not correct, if one really wants to investigate changes in the purchasing power of the worker, to assume that the workers' standard, aside from changing customs and fashions, remains always the same. While it may be right to measure wages during times of prosperity by changes in the prices of a budget based on a "health and decency standard," this standard undoubtedly is very far from reality in times of depression.

All these considerations lead to the conclusion that an adequate index of the cost of living should have its composition changed almost yearly. This means that one should understand by cost of living not the cost of a fixed standard of living, but of a mode of living changing according to changes in wages and their purchasing power. We really can measure changes in the cost of living only after we already have measured the changes of living ; we cannot construct an adequate workers' budget as basis for a cost-of-living index before we know how the purchasing power of wages has changed the workers' mode of living.

The ideal way of measuring what we mean to measure by the construction of an index of the cost of living would be to compute a real wage index with the help of a cost-of-living index, based on annually changing budgets, the monthly figures of two succeeding years being linked according to the chain index method.

But the data available for the construction of such a series of budgets are still utterly inadequate, and for the present we cannot do without the construction of the usual index of real wages.

But even the figures available for the construction of such an index of real wages are very untrustworthy. The computations, as such, of the official index numbers of the cost of living for England or France or Germany or the U.S.A., are correct. But they fail, on the one hand, to take into account so many necessary expenditures and, on the other hand, they credit the worker with so many purchases for which he has no money that very much could and should be done to improve them.

This applies even more to cost-of-living indices going back before the War, covering the nineteenth and the first years of the twentieth centuries.

.   .   .   .   .   .

While real wages are computed to indicate changes in absolute labour conditions, relative wages should be a measure of changes in relative labour conditions.

For about 100 years economists made comparisons of

changes in wages and in prices without, however, computing an index of real wages. Real wages were computed only towards the end of the nineteenth century, and only with the price increases caused by the War did the interest in and the computation of real wages become more general.

The ideas underlying the computation of relative wages are almost as old, and already Marx has made many pertinent remarks about the relative movement of wages and production. But the first computation of relative wages were not made until 1927, and even to-day they arouse very little interest.

Relative wages are wages which show the relative movement of the purchasing power of the worker on the one hand, and the relative movement of the purchasing power of the rest of society on the other hand.

If production increases more than the purchasing power of the workers their relative position is quite obviously growing worse because they can buy only a smaller share of the national product. If, on the other hand, the purchasing power of the worker increases more than national production then quite obviously the share of the worker in national production is increasing.

In order to compute relative wages we must first define national production. Does national production mean the national production of consumption goods, or the total national production ? At first sight the answer seems to be : only the production of consumption goods can be meant, because the worker buys only consumption goods. Such a conclusion would, however, lead to the following difficulties. In capitalist society there exists a tendency to accumulate capital. By capital we do not mean money but goods which are used for production. Such goods, such capital, are factories, machines, etc. With the help of this capital the employer engages workers and makes profits. For the employer capital goods, then, are most important as a help to make profits. Let us assume the employers decide to stabilize the production of consumption goods at a certain level and concentrate for a time chiefly on a big increase in the production of production goods. Production as a whole, let us say, would increase by 30 per cent, wages by 10 per cent, and prices would remain the same. Then, necessarily the purchasing power of the worker would be higher by 10 per cent in relation to the sum of consumption goods. Relative wages, if defined as the relation between purchasing power and the total production of consumption goods, would increase—while in fact the relative position of the worker would not only not improve but would deteriorate since the employers are building up a mighty accumulation of capital in which the workers have no share.

In calculating relative wages it is, therefore, necessary to relate the purchasing power of the worker on the one side to the total national product on the other side.

Since purchasing power (real wages) is an economic factor independent of the movement of prices, production, if related to purchasing power, has to be made independent of prices too. The simplest way of doing this is to compute an index of the physical volume of production.

One must, however, keep in mind that by far the greater part of the national product is bought at wholesale prices. It is, therefore, necessary to take into account the difference between the movement of wholesale prices, and that of retail prices at which the worker buys. This we can do by dividing the index of retail prices by the index of wholesale prices and by multiplying the index of the physical volume of production by the result of the division of the two price indices.

Since we compare the purchasing power of the average individual worker we must compute also an index of production per person. Since we ascertain the relative position of the worker in economic society we must compare the purchasing power of the individual worker with the volume of production per member of that society, per person living in England or in France, etc., if translated into national terms.

Many minor factors have to be taken into account. The most important among them is the difference between imports and exports.

The purchasing power of the worker should be computed in the following way. We begin by calculating net wages. These we contrast with an index of retail prices. This index of retail prices should be constructed quite differently from an index of the cost of living. For we are not interested in comparing the development of wages with the development of the prices of those commodities which the worker buys, but with the development of the prices of any commodity which the worker could buy on the retail market, that is with all retail commodities. The price index which we use to correct net money wages should, therefore, include all commodities on the retail market and be an index of the general retail price level. The result of the division of the index of net money wages by the index of general retail prices is an index of the purchasing power of the worker on the total retail market.

If we now divide this corrected index of net " real " wages by the index of the national product we arrive at an index of the relative position of the worker which is identical with the index of relative wages.*

The formula is : Index of :

$$\text{Relative Wages} = \frac{\substack{\text{Net Wages per} \\ \text{Worker}}}{\substack{\text{General Retail} \\ \text{Prices}}} : \left(\substack{\text{National} \\ \text{per} \\ \text{capita} \\ \text{Product}} \times \frac{\substack{\text{General Retail} \\ \text{Prices}}}{\substack{\text{General Whole-} \\ \text{sale Prices}}} \right)$$

This formula is by no means accurate since it does not include, for instance, changes in the national product caused by exports and imports. And yet a further simplification is necessary : since for no country a general retail price index is available, it will have to be replaced by a cost-of-living index. The formula then runs : Index of :

$$\text{Relative Wages} = \substack{\text{Net Real Wage} \\ \text{per} \\ \text{Worker}} : \left(\substack{\text{National} \\ \text{per capita} \\ \text{Product}} \times \frac{\text{Cost of Living}}{\text{Wholesale Prices}} \right)$$

With this formula it is possible to compute a very rough index of relative wages for many decades back.†

* After the discussion on " pitfalls of averages " it is only necessary to point out here that a much more useful index of relative wages could be constructed by passing the national boundaries and extending the investigation, for example, to English economic society as a whole.

† For a more comprehensive explanation of relative wages compare, *Der Anteil des deutschen Industriearbeiters am Sozialprodukt—Zum Problem des relativen Verelendung* by Jürgen Kuczynski, in *Kölner Sozialpolitische Vierteljahresschrift*, X. Jahrgang, Heft 1, and Jürgen Kuczynski, *Die Entwicklung der Lage der Arbeiterschaft in Europa und Amerika*, 1870–1933.

4. ON CERTAIN " LAWS OF WAGES "

The observer of short-range and long-range wage statistics will find certain movements and tendencies which are repeated so often in the history of wages that it is safe to speak of them as laws of wages. By laws we must understand certain regularities of movement, certain tendencies which determine the course of wages, even though they are not always revealed openly because certain other tendencies are stronger, and, therefore, more effective.

As far as short-range wage movements are concerned the most important " habits " of wages are :

Money wages and real wages increase during times of prosperity.

Money wages decrease during times of crisis and depression.

Money wages and real wage indices which take into account losses through unemployment, etc., decrease during times of crisis and depression.

Relative wages increase during times of crisis and depression. This increase does not mean an absolute improvement of labour conditions since the share of the workers is increased only while the total national product is declining. The greater share per worker (the increased relative wage) is absolutely smaller during the depression than the smaller share during the period of prosperity.

Relative wages decrease during times of prosperity.

All regularities of short-range movements are connected with and caused by the general cyclical movements of capitalist economy.

There are no "long waves" or secular movements or "long-range business cycles."* And yet there are certain regularities in the long-range movement of wages.

These regularities are accounted for and explained by certain features which are inherent in the growth of any capitalist society.

Two of these features are the relative development of industry and agriculture, and the difference between agricultural and industrial wages. Growing capitalist structure means growing industrialization of a country. Growing

* I investigated the long-range movement of prices and production in *Das Problem der langen Wellen und die Entwicklung der Industire-waren-Preise in den Jahren*, 1820–1933, Basel, 1934, and *Weltproduktion und Welthandel in den letzten 100 Jahren*, Liepaja, 1935.

industrialization means increasing weight of industry and decreasing weight of agriculture within an economic society. Increasing weight of industry means increasing weight of relatively higher wages. For industry always pays more than agriculture, and if that part of economic society which, on the average, pays higher wages is employing more and more workers then, of course, the average wage of all workers has a tendency to increase.

Without wage increases for individual industries or occupations, wages in growing capitalist societies show a tendency to increase, because of the general shift of workers from agriculture to industry.

A very similar law can be formulated for industry alone. Growing capitalism is accompanied by a relative increase of the production of production goods. Iron and steel industries are gaining upon textiles. Now iron and steel industries pay a higher wage than the textile industries.

Again we find that without wage increases by individual industries or occupations the average wage for industry as a whole has a tendency to increase, because of the general shift of workers from the lower-paying textile industries to the higher-paying iron and steel industries.

These tendencies of long-range wage statistics very rarely are counterbalanced or outbalanced by other tendencies during the time of quickly growing capitalism.

But during the period of the general crisis of capitalism, since about the end of the nineteenth century in England, and a somewhat later date in other countries, new factors have become effective.

Agriculture is losing only little in relative importance, industrial capacity begins to outgrow industrial production and very severe crises are depressing chiefly the industries producing production goods. There are years during which the relative importance of agriculture and of consumption industries is not only not declining, but increases slightly. And the number of these years is increasing in the course of time and becoming large enough to outweigh for a certain time all the other tendencies mentioned before.

While one may say, therefore, that there is a long-range tendency for wages to increase during years and decades of growing capitalism, that is, during the nineteenth century in the big capitalist countries, this long-range tendency has been weakened very much, but probably has not been wiped out during the period of the general crisis of capitalism, that is, for the big capitalist countries, during the twentieth century.

It is obvious that the long-range tendency of wages to increase may find expression in an actual increase of wages as well as in stagnation (while wages in individual occupations are declining), or in a decrease of wages (which is slighter than the decrease by occupations). In a later chapter we shall try to show, however, that even an increase of wages does not necessarily mean an improvement of labour conditions.

Relative wages have the long-range tendency to decrease, and are very rarely affected by counter-tendencies at whatever period in the development of capitalism.

5. LIMITS OF STATISTICAL EXPRESSION

The ideal way to express statistically the movement of wages is, of course, the computation of one single index showing the trend of wages under the combined influence of all pertinent factors.

This ideal, however, cannot be realized. There is, at present at least, no way to express at one and the same time the movement of real wages and the movement of relative wages. All formulas I have tried lead to a nonsensical mixture of trends which very often cancel each other.

It is, therefore, necessary to compute at least two indices : the one shows the development of absolute wage conditions while the other traces the development of relative wage conditions.

But even these two indices are not enough.

On the face of it, the trend of average wages may, for two given samples, be the same, and yet be intrinsically different. An average increase (or decrease) may be the result of a general increase (decrease) or of increases (decreases) compensated in part by decreases (increases). No one probably would call these changes in labour conditions identical, or would say that labour conditions have improved equally if wages for all occupations have increased by 3 per cent, and if wages have increased in some occupations by 5 and more per cent while they have decreased in others.

Probably most statisticians would say that labour is better off if wages increase at about the same rate in all occupations than if wages increase considerably in some while they decrease in others. This, naturally, leads to the conclusion that it is not sufficient to observe only the trend of wages for all the workers combined, but that it is necessary also to split up the general average and to observe the movement of wages by industrial subgroups.

Very probably such an investigation of subgroups will permit us to make a final estimate of the nature of the movement of wages. But it is also possible that such an investigation will lead to no result. Let us assume, for instance, that wages of all workers have increased by 5 per cent in one country, and by 6 per cent in another country. At first sight one would say that wage conditions in the latter country have improved more. But let us assume further that the 5 per cent increase in the former country is the result of changes in individual industries fluctuating between 3 and 7 per cent, while the 6 per cent increase in the other country is the result of changes in individual industries ranging from a 10 per cent decrease to a 15 per cent increase of wages. I doubt if a final decision could be arrived at and be generally concurred in : as to which country experienced the greater improvement of wage conditions, the country with the somewhat greater average increase but with industries showing wage decreases, or the one with the somewhat smaller average increase but without any industry showing a wage decrease.

The limits of statistical expression are considerable. On the one hand, it is impossible to express wage conditions in one single index. On the other hand, it is doubtful in certain cases whether wage statistics, even if they are split up for purposes of more thorough investigation, can lead to any final conclusion at all about comparative wage conditions.

II. WAGES AND LABOUR CONDITIONS

After having examined wages and their characteristics, the question arises as to how far wages can be used as an indicator of labour conditions.

It is a well-known fact that money wages are not sufficient

D

for this purpose. In order to investigate changes in absolute labour conditions it is necessary—as has been universally recognized—to compute real wage statistics.

Indices of real wages enable us to investigate changes in the purchasing power of the worker. The question which we have to answer now is : do changes in the purchasing power alone determine labour conditions ? Does an increase in the purchasing power of the worker of, for instance, 10 per cent mean that labour conditions have improved ? Does a decrease by 10 per cent mean that labour conditions have deteriorated ? And have they improved, or deteriorated to the same extent as the purchasing power has increased or decreased ? Briefly : are real wages sufficient as a measuring-rod of absolute labour conditions ?

Such questions are generally most difficult to answer ; a great mass of statistical material must be collected, and very often the material gathered with much trouble proves to be insufficient or, at best, inconclusive.

In this case, however, it is comparatively easy to answer such a question—owing to the needs and diligence of military organization.

.   .   .   .

If we examine the general movement of real wages in England during the nineteenth and the twentieth century we find few periods during which real wages increased at the rate which characterize the eighties and nineties of the last century.

Now, at the beginning of this century military authorities, on looking back over the last ten to twenty years of the preceding century, grew alarmed and startled non-labour circles in England with the contention that the working-class population, from which most of the recruits were drawn, was in a process of physical deterioration.

Major-General H. C. Borrett, Inspector-General of Recruiting wrote in his Annual Report for 1902, as follows :*

" The one subject which causes anxiety in the future as regards recruiting is the gradual deterioration of the physique of the working-classes, from whom the bulk of the recruits

* *Report of the Inter-Departmental Committee on Physical Deterioration* Vol. II, p. 7.

must always be drawn. When it is remembered that recruiters
are instructed not to submit for medical examination candi-
dates for enlistment unless they are reasonably expected to
be passed as fit, one cannot but be struck by the percentage
considered by the medical officers as unfit for the service."

Much discussion arose and an Inter-Departmental Committee on Physical Deterioration was formed " to make a
preliminary enquiry into the allegations concerning the
deterioration of certain classes of the population as shown
by the large percentage of rejections for physical causes of
recruits for the Army and by other evidence, especially the
*Report of the Royal Commission on Physical Training (Scot-
land)* . . . "*

Much evidence was heard, many authorities were ques-
tioned, and although some members of the commission were
prejudiced, as is shown by the formulation of the questions,
and did not want to believe in physical deterioration, the
most important witnesses either did not find any improvement of conditions during the period of rising real wages
or even many signs of deterioration.

We shall quote only two of the numerous witnesses. They
were, undoubtedly, the best equipped to judge and are, to
this day, regarded not only as the greatest authorities on
the subject during that time, but also as men cautious in
giving final judgments. The two witnesses are Charles Booth
and Seebohm Rowntree.

The Minutes of evidence† on the examination of Booth
read :

" (*Chairman.*) You are the author of *Life and Labour in
London,* are you not ?—I am.

" Did your investigations produce the impression that
conditions unfavourable to the health of the community
were growing in intensity ?—I think I should not use the
word ' intensity.' They are growing in amount in connection
with the increase of the urban conditions of life. I could
not say that the conditions have been more intense, but they
are more widespread."

Booth is of the opinion that living conditions of the
working class have not deteriorated (neither have they
improved in his opinion) but that unfavourable conditions

* *Report*, Vol. I, p. v.
† *Report*, Vol. II, p. 47.

prevailing in some places a number of years ago, have spread to many more places. Thus there was no increase in deterioration as far as those parts of the working class which were worst off a number of years ago are concerned ; but since more and more members of the working class had been drawn down to the level of the worst group average living conditions among workers had deteriorated.

The evidence of Mr. Rowntree runs as follows : *

" (*Chairman.*) You are the author of the book upon the conditions of life and labour in York ?—Yes.

" Therefore you have made some considerable study of the conditions of the problems which we are asked to investigate ?—Yes, a very fair amount.

" Are you in a position to say anything on the general question as to whether the conditions that make for deteriorated physique are increasing in intensity, or otherwise ? —I do not think that I have any scientific information on the point. I have a general opinion that the conditions are such that it must be so. There is a greater proportion of people living in towns."

Although very cautious in expressing his opinion and very candid as to the scientific value of the premises on which he would base his opinion, Mr. Rowntree does not hesitate to assert that conditions making for physical deterioration of the working class are becoming more widespread and more forceful.

.   .   .   .   .   .

The above evidence helps us to realize a fact partly known already, especially at a time when wage statistics were not yet much used as evidence about the development of labour conditions : an index of wages, though a very important indicator of the trend of labour conditions, gives by no means sufficient proof of the trend of labour conditions. Other factors affect labour conditions to a high degree, and the effect of increasing real wages upon general labour conditions can very well be offset by other factors influencing labour conditions in the opposite direction. An increase of real wages is by no means a sure sign for an improvement in labour conditions, and labour conditions do not change in exact proportion to variations in real wages.

* *Report*, Vol. II, p. 200.

A general judgment as to whether labour conditions are improving or deteriorating must take into consideration many factors. And quite often these factors may not even have a direct bearing on labour conditions.

For the different business-cycles during the last 120 years all the evidence available points to the fact that labour conditions improve absolutely during the period of prosperity. That holds true of the cycles in the beginning of the last century as well as of the business-cycles during this century. As to the trend of labour conditions during a period of crisis the very opposite can be observed with equal certainty and regularity. Even a rough survey will reveal this.

The case is quite different and much more complex when we compare, for instance, labour conditions during the peak of any upswing with labour conditions during the peak of any other, former or later, upswing. Then, as many factors influencing labour conditions as possible must be investigated, and real wages alone are quite inadequate as the sole measuring-rod of labour conditions. Even so, it seems quite safe to assume that labour conditions have deteriorated if real wages have decreased. But, on the other hand, one cannot be certain that labour conditions have improved if real wages have increased.

Why this difference between declining and increasing real wages as indicators of the trend of labour conditions ? If such a difference really obtains, it would necessarily follow that there is a tendency for all other factors influencing labour conditions (taken together) to develop in such a way as to impair labour conditions. An investigation of labour conditions would then have to start with the following assumption:

With the exception of wages all factors influencing labour conditions have, in their entirety (not necessarily each of them always), the tendency to affect labour conditions unfavourably. Therefore, we must put the question : if real wages increase, do all other factors taken together more than compensate for this increase and in the end worsen labour conditions, or do they not over-compensate the increase in purchasing power, and labour conditions improve or remain at least unchanged ?

Two problems have then to be investigated : firstly the problem of the tendency of all non-wage factors to influence labour conditions and, secondly, the relative importance of these non-wage factors as compared with the influence of the wage factor itself.

.   .   .   .   .   .

Capitalist enterprise is run for profit. Profits increase with increasing returns from the worker. Increasing returns from the worker—assuming wages and prices to remain stationary—can be brought about by forcing labour to greater exertion, by increasing the intensity of the work done by the worker.*

In capitalist society, there exists therefore a tendency to enhance the working intensity. The effect on labour conditions is unfavourable. Increased intensity of work undermines the health of the worker, makes it neccessary for him to eat better and to sleep more, and to have more recreation in order to be able to keep up the pace.

In time, labour conditions would, other things remaining equal, become unbearable for the working class owing to increasing intensity of work. Therefore—as happens in times of improving business conditions—the employers are obliged to better labour conditions in some way, either by paying higher real wages, or by shortening the hours of work, or by improving housing conditions, or by providing some recreational facilities, in order to be able to keep the intensity of work at the high level reached or to push it even farther.

Intensity of work is the most important factor influencing the trend of capitalist society. Introduction of and improvements in machinery are the basis of industrial progress. Increasing intensity is the basis of increasing profits (if real wages are not be decreased). Profits can, of course, also be added to by decreasing the purchasing power of the worker, and for three decades this has been done as it had been done also from time to time during the previous century. But since employers know at least as much of

* The intensity of the work was during the first third of the nineteenth century increased partly by extending the working day and, later on, almost exclusively by increasing the amount of work done per hour.

human psychology as anybody else, they prefer the less risky way of swelling profits by enhancing the intensity of work.

Improvements in individual labour conditions alleviating to some extent the effects of increasing intensity of work imply a relative decrease of profits. Rather than decrease the intensity of work, employers prefer to alleviate some of the bad effects of that intensity by improving labour conditions in some other way. A continuous increase of the intensity of work assures the employers, to a certain degree, of a continuous increase in production. This continuous increase of production assures the employer of a continuous accumulation of the means for running capitalist enterprise, of a continuous increase of the means of production, of a continuous increase of the means of employing labour and of profiting from this employment. Since only this continuous increase of the accumulation of means of production used for employing labour, assures the employer of a continuously expanding utilization of his source of profits— the labour force employed—it is obvious that employers will rather consider any measure for keeping the labour force fit for continued work, than a decrease in the intensity of work.

But since, at the same time, capitalist society is progressing only if profits increase, it is reasonable to assume that all alleviations the employing class has applied—decrease in the number of hours of work, social insurance, extension of recreational facilities, etc.—have cost the employers less than a decrease of the intensity of work would have cost them. Or, from the worker's standpoint : all improvements in labour conditions have brought him less in value than the increasing intensity of work costs him.

Capitalist society is run for the greatest possible profit. The greatest possible profit can only be achieved by keeping wages as low as possible and working intensity as high as possible. Since the worker's place in the employer's production scheme is that of a producing machine combining cheapest possible cost with the highest possible efficiency all living facilities provided by the employer for the worker are only intended to keep him fit as a working and profit-producing machine. Since profits should always be as high as possible it would be a sign of inefficient management to spend more on the compensation of the ill-effects of increasing intensity of work than is absolutely necessary. The tendency, on the contrary, is to increase the intensity of work at as little cost as possible.

The cost saving may be effected, for instance, by increasing real wages rather than introducing a social insurance system (see the development of real wages in the United States during the last forty years), or it may be accomplished by initiating a system of social insurance, and decreasing at the same time real wages (see the development of real wages in Germany during the last thirty years), or it may be arrived at by increasing real wages and by disregarding, among others, the more and more pressing problem of housing the worker (see England during the latter half of the nineteenth century), or in many other ways.

The analyst of labour conditions under the capitalist system past and present, must therefore tackle an absolutely different task than he seemed to face at the beginning of this discussion. His aim should not be to discuss whether or not other factors compensate, or more than offset, an increase in real wages. But his problem is : which means do, and did, the employing class use to alleviate some of the ill-effects of increasing intensity of work in order to continue and increase the present exploitation?

The only individual factor of whose trend we can always be certain is the working intensity. It is always increasing. Most other factors are merely results of the movement of different costs of alleviative programmes. Under certain conditions employers choose to increase real wages ; under other conditions they prefer to decrease real wages, but provide some means of support for the unemployed.

Since labour conditions are continuously deteriorating—not from year to year, for they undoubtedly improve during times of prosperity, but from business-cycle to business-cycle—the investigation of labour conditions is, as we pointed out already, chiefly concerned with the various factors influencing labour conditions, and tries to ascertain which of them moved which way during which period, and which of them that way during that period. It is no longer an investigation of the trend of labour conditions, but of the trend of the individual factors which, in their entirety, worsen labour conditions, but which, taken individually, may and

do improve certain aspects of labour conditions, different
aspects at different times.

.   .   .   .   .   .

In any appraisal of labour conditions the problem of
wages would then seem to have become a comparatively un-
important one, no more and no less important than, let us
say, the problem of housing conditions. This, however, is
not true. Wages must be singled out as the most important
individual factor influencing labour conditions, working
intensity excepted. Since working intensity is increasing
continuously, it is obvious that labour conditions are
deteriorating at an especially rapid pace if real wages
decrease at the same time. And labour conditions are
deteriorating very probably less quickly, if real wages
improve.

The conclusion must be drawn : though wages are, by
themselves, insufficient as an indicator of labour conditions,
they are fully adequate to indicate the pace in the changes
of labour conditions. If real wages increase from business-
cycle to business-cycle, one may assume with certainty that
the pace of deterioration of labour conditions has become
slower, while a decrease of real wages (from business-cycle
to business-cycle) indicates a quickening of the pace of the
deterioration of labour conditions.

.   .   .   .   .   .

Of course, all the deductions we drew from the profit
motive of capitalist society pertain only to capitalist society
as a whole, or rather to any capitalist organism. They do
not pertain to isolated regions. It is, for instance, quite
thinkable that labour conditions in England may have
improved during some business-cycles (and they certainly
have deteriorated relatively less) at the expense of the
Indian worker, the South African negro, or any other group
of workers employed by English capitalists outside of
England.

If one wants to investigate, therefore, whether labour
conditions in English capitalist society have deteriorated at
a quicker pace in the twentieth century than in the second
half of the nineteenth century, it would not be sufficient

to investigate the development of labour conditions in England alone, but one would have to add an examination of labour conditions in Ireland, in India, in South Africa, briefly, in fact, in all the places where English capital is employing labour.

III. LABOUR CONDITIONS

The only factor continuously making labour conditions worse, seems to be the increase in the intensity of work.

There are no statistics available for measuring the increase in the intensity of work. It is difficult enough to measure the increase in the hourly productive capacity of the worker ; but to dissect this increase and to find out how much of it is due to improvements in machinery or to improvements in the organization of the production process, and how much is due to increased exertion on the part of the worker, is absolutely impossible without a far more detailed knowledge of the production process than we have to-day.

The enormous increase of the intensity of work, especially in present times, can, however, be gauged from many descriptions of industrial work. To-day many industrial concerns run a department whose sole task it is to find out ways and means of increasing the intensity of work. The tendency has gone even farther. Not only the intensity of work in the concern as a whole is being increased, but also the intensity of work in the department finding means to quicken the working pitch in the factory as a whole.

The *Preliminary Report on Study of Regularization of Employment and Improvement of Labor Conditions in the Automobile Industry* gives the following description :*

" The (automobile) industry led the country in effective time-study of its operations and the time-study men gradually brought its operations to this efficient peak. The competitive conditions of the past few years have reached down to these time-study men. They have been forced to show how to make inequitable reductions in working time to hold their own jobs, and, from setting jobs on an efficient basis, they have come to set them on a speed-up basis that puts pro-

* Prepared and published by the National Recovery Administration, Research and Planning Division, p. 46.

duction demands beyond human capability to produce day after day."

.   .   .   .   .   .

The most important other factor influencing labour conditions is the real wage. By real wages we understand here full-time weekly real wages.

The last decades especially have revealed the significance of a third factor : short-time and unemployment. This factor has always played an important rôle during times of crisis and depression. Only after the World War, after the world crisis of 1920–2 this factor has acquired great weight also in times of increasing business activity. During all the years since 1920–2, when production was rising, unemployment has remained at a high level in the three most important capitalist countries : in England, and in the United States, and in Germany. During these years probably no individual factor influencing labour conditions has so much contributed to lower the standard of living of the working class as the extent of short-time and unemployment.

In combination with the trend of full-time weekly real wages they have worsened labour conditions to such a degree that—the simultaneous increase in the intensity of work being kept in mind—no further evidence is needed to show that the standard of living of the worker has declined quite seriously in post-War years, much more so than during most of the former business-cycles.

By calculating their influence on wages it is comparatively easy to demonstrate most of the effects of unemployment and short-time on the standard of living of the worker. Some of the effects, however, cannot be shown so easily. The experience of the last two years, during which employment began to rise again in a number of countries, has taught us :

(1). That accidents among newly employed workers are very much higher than among those workers who were continuously at their jobs.

(2). That the efficiency of the newly employed workers is very much lower than that of the others (though they work with a much greater subjective intensity in order to keep their jobs).

(3). That they have forgotten, or not yet learned, many

methods of production, and must often start all anew in certain lines of production in which they were formerly masters.

Many of these points can find expression in corrected real wage statistics. But the gnawing fear of losing the job and the wearing tension of their efforts cannot be expressed statistically.

The same holds true of the similar fear of the workers still employed during times of crisis and depression who are daily in danger of losing their jobs. We find a description of the mental anguish these workers suffer in the Preliminary Report on Study of Regularization of Employment and Improvement of Labor Conditions in the Automobile Industry :*

" One of the psychological problems faced by the automobile worker to-day is the gamble that he knows he is facing as he goes to work each day. He sees the men waiting at the gate for an interview for employment. If he is feeling badly on a particular day and slows down in his gait, his straw-boss or foreman tells him, ' Step on it. If you don't want the job, there are thousands outside who do,' or ' Look out the window and see the men waiting in line for your job.' "

Not in every factory is the worker made to realize in such a drastic way the precariousness of his position, the insecurity of his job. Even so, the worker knows how "lucky" he is to be still at work, is uncomfortable day after day, unhappy and miserable because of his constant fear of losing his job.

It is obvious that this fear cannot be stated quantitatively, and that it is therefore impossible to find an exact evaluation for the development of labour conditions. All statistical expressions, all figures are only approximations, and do not take into account many factors contributing their share to the deterioration (or to the alleviation of the bad effects of deteriorating labour conditions).

.　　.　　.　　.　　.　　.

Next to unemployment and short-time, social insurance institutions are probably the most important factor influenc-

* *Report*, p. 51.

ing labour conditions. Social insurance is a comparatively new palliative applied by employers with the intention of improving certain aspects of labour conditions.

The most notable kinds of social insurance are : old-age insurance, health insurance, unemployment insurance, and accident insurance.

Social insurance lessens the bad effects of many factors influencing labour conditions. Unemployment insurance attenuates the consequences of growing unemployment for the worker's wage income. Accident insurance moderates the results of the worker's inability to make his living. Old-age insurance lessens the effects of growing natural physical inability to work upon the worker's standard of living, and health insurance those of illness upon the purchasing power of the worker.

The introduction of social insurance undoubtedly brings advantages to the worker. The advantage does not only lie in the benefits the worker derives from the introduction of the system but also in the permanency of the system. Social insurance is introduced only if, firstly, the effects of certain factors influencing labour conditions have become so detrimental to the producing ability of the worker that capitalist society is obliged to alleviate labour conditions somewhat in order to keep the worker physically fit to continue work at the high standard of intensity prevailing ; or even in order to increase still further the working intensity, and if, secondly, it is preferable from the capitalist point of view to introduce a social insurance system rather than to increase real wages or to apply some other palliative.

Social insurance has one great advantage for the employers. It regularizes the ministration of treatments of the working class against certain evils. Unemployment insurance, for instance, regularizes the prophylactic treatment against certain ill-effects of unemployment. It regularizes the relief work, it spreads the costs of unemployment relief over the nation as a whole, and helps those sections of the country, or those industries, which suffer particularily from unemployment by compelling other sections and other industries, which suffer less or not at all from unemployment to contribute to the general unemployment fund.

Expressed in monetary terms the introduction of a social

insurance system probably means no very great additional burden for the capitalists, and probably none for the workers, taking into account, of course, the benefit payments to the workers.

The advantages of social insurance to the worker are several. On the one hand it makes it easier for the worker to get relief (some at least he got also before from local or private benefit funds), the administration of relief is quicker, smoother and reaches a greater number of workers ; and very probably he gets more support than before.

The other great advantage for the workers lies in a certain permanency of the insurance mechanism. If employers decide to raise real wages as a palliative against the growing ill-effects of other factors influencing labour conditions it is comparatively easy for them to switch over to some other method of combating some of the evils of labour conditions ; they may, for instance, decide to decrease real wages and to improve housing conditions. But, once introduced, social insurance can be " curtailed " only with comparative difficulty as was shown by the attempts, during the last crisis, to decrease benefits and to reduce the number of those entitled to benefits. True, the employers were able to impose new limitations, but they were, for instance, much more successful in decreasing real wages than in restricting social insurance benefits.

On the other hand, the advantages of social insurance must not be over-estimated. It is by no means a rare thing that the workers decline the benefits of social insurance or social legislation because these benefits are " disadvantageous " to the worker under present conditions.

Two examples are sufficient to show why such cases occur. The one pertains to the child-labour legislation in the southern states of the United States of America. During the 'twenties some of the southern states began to introduce certain laws and factory rules forbidding the employment of children below a certain age. Most of the employers as well as most of the parents were against this innovation. Again and again factory inspectors found themselves confronted by a united front of parents and employers when they tried to enforce the statutes. The reason was a very simple one : the wages of the parents were so low that they could not raise a family without the additional cents earned by their children. At the very point where the wages of the parents were sufficient to raise a family at least on the standard of an existence minimum, the front lines ran quite differently, and the parents opposed the employers.

A second example may be taken from conditions in Germany. The reports of factory inspectors in Germany complain year after year that pregnant women do not avail themselves of the opportunity of leaving the factory a few weeks before childbirth and of staying away from their work a few weeks after the confinement, even if they get compensation. The reason is again a very simple one. The compensation they receive is not as high as their wage, and they cannot lose even a part of their wage because it is small enough already. And since the compensation is based on the wages earned during the weeks just preceding the retiring period, one often finds that these women never work as hard as during these very weeks in order to get —in case they are physically compelled to retire—a compensation based on as high a wage as possible.

Both these examples show that social insurance and social benefit systems are sometimes (but in the minority of cases) of very little use to the worker, because the worker whose wages are too low cannot avail himself of the advantages offered.

.   .   .   .

Health conditions, or rather the influence of working conditions upon health are another most important factor whose relevance is by no means recognized in its entire scope. While the influence of home conditions upon the health of the worker has been acknowledged for quite a long time—not so the whole of the influence of shop conditions.

With the rapid and widespread growth of cities home conditions have become a prominent feature of health legislation. And there can be no doubt that the betterment in the health of the population has been extraordinary. Contagious diseases of a serious nature have decreased considerably. The death-rate has gone down greatly. Housing conditions have improved.

Some of this progress the worker occasionally has heavily

paid for. Measures for the protection of health have sometimes only led to further deterioration of health. The most
interesting illustration during recent years is furnished by
the anti-slum campaign in England. Undoubtedly the
extension of slums has been checked in post-War times,
and many workers live in better homes to-day than thirty
years ago. But on the other side rents have gone up to such
a degree that many workers are obliged to cut their food
budget in order to pay the rent : they live in better rooms
but are more undernourished than before.

Allen Hutt in his book *The Condition of the Working Class
in Britain*, writes :*

" This [the effect of the burden of high rents on health]
has received its most remarkable demonstration in the
observations conducted during the past five years by Dr.
M'Gonigle, the medical officer of health of Stockton-on-Tees.

" Dr. M'Gonigle, in a paper read to the Royal Society of
Medicine, has explained that during this period the death-
rate of a number of families re-housed on a new Council
estate rose by 8.47 per thousand, while the death-rate of
families remaining in slum conditions fell by 2.9 per thousand :

" ' On analysing this surprising situation, he found that
the transfer had involved an increase in rent from 9s. to
13s. 4¾d. weekly, and even with some sharing of houses the
re-housed unemployed were left with only 36.7 per cent of
their income available for food. Their diet showed all-round
deficiencies ; fat, for example, was 34 per cent short of normal
needs. He could find no explanation of the poor health and
increased mortality of this population except that the higher
rent left them unsufficient money to buy enough food.
(*Week-end Review*, March 11th, 1933.)' "

This example is very similar to those we cited for child-
labour legislation in the United States, and legislation for
pregnant women in Germany. It shows that measures applied
to alleviate the bad effects of certain factors influencing
labour conditions sometimes do not benefit the worker at
all, because other factors (mostly low wages) do not permit
these restorative means to function unhampered.

But just as it would be stupid to deny the good effects
of social insurance because sometimes it is ineffective, it
would be nonsensical to fight against slum clearance and

* p. viii.

better housing. In such cases emphasis must be laid upon the removal of those factors which obstruct the successful application of the alleviating measures.

The ill-effects of health conditions in the factory and on the way to the factory are at least as important ; but their influence on labour conditions is much underrated. True, something has been done to improve health conditions in factories, especially in connection with accident insurance and the reduction of illnesses due to certain working processes, chiefly of those demanding the manipulation of certain chemicals and metals.

But how much more is there still to be done! The deplorable effects of bad working conditions and probably also of unhealthy conditions of transport from the house to the working place and back again have been revealed during the present crisis.

Never during the industrial history of the last 150 years has unemployment been as high as during the last years. And never have health conditions among workers been better than during this crisis. This holds true for the United States as well as England and Germany, or any other country where unemployment is high.

Increasing unemployment has been accompanied by a general improvement of health and an unusually declining death-rate. A seemingly impossible situation has developed : while workers and their families often had to scrape together their last pennies in order not to die of hunger, their health improved.

But to conclude from this that it is better for workers to be hungry and that hunger improves health, would be just as unreasonable as to conclude from the example given above, that to live in slums is good for the health of the workers.

Rather, the conclusion to be drawn is : the lack of food and all the other factors which are injurious to the unemployed worker's health are overcompensated by the fact that this unemployed worker is no longer exposed to all the health hazards on his way to the factory, within the factory, and on his way home from the factory. The detrimental effect of working conditions must indeed be enormous to be offset by the one fact that the unemployed worker does

E

not go to work, and while he suffers from so many ills which trouble the employed worker little or not at all.

It is very difficult to measure what it means for the worker's health not to go to work. Among the best statistics for the purpose are the German statistics of the number of days of illness per person insured against sickness. Since the unemployed also remains insured these figures pertain to all workers.*

Year	Number of Days of Illness per Insured Member	Percentage of Unemployment
1924	10.8	12.8
1925	12.5	6.2
1926	12.0	19.1
1927	12.9	9.6
1928	13.6	9.0
1929	14.0	13.7
1930	10.7	23.4
1931	11.6	36.2
1932	9.2	46.8

Generally, while unemployment is high the number of days of illness decreases, and while unemployment is comparatively low the number of days of illness increases.

Our interpretation might be challenged as follows : if unemployment is high the worker is afraid to stay at home in spite of feeling ill, because he may lose his job. Therefore, illness may very well increase with rising unemployment while the figures show a falling off in the number of days of illness per worker. This explanation is partially true. No doubt, the worker is even more reluctant to stay away from his job during times of crisis and depression, than during times of increasing business activity, however ill he may be.

But though the worker may go to his factory even if he is very ill, though he may overcome by sheer will-power many effects of his illness, and thus vitiate the meaning of statistics of illness per member of the sickness-insurance system, he cannot vitiate death statistics.

And death statistics, just as well as health statistics, indicate an improvement during times of increasing unemployment.

* Cf., *Statistisches Jahrbuch für das Deutsche Reich.*

The death-rate developed in Germany as follows for men
between the ages of 20 and 60 :*

Death per 1,000 Men, 1924–32

Age	1924–6	1927	1928	1929	1930	1931	1932
20–25	4.5	4.0	4.1	4.1	3.6	3.2	3.0
25–30	4.2	4.0	3.9	4.0	3.6	3.3	3.1
30–35	4.1	3.9	4.0	4.3	3.9	3.7	3.4
35–40	4.7	4.7	4.5	4.9	4.6	4.3	4.1
40–45	6.1	6.1	5.9	6.3	5.7	5.6	5.3
45–50	8.3	8.4	8.3	8.8	7.9	7.8	7.3
50–55	12.1	12.2	12.0	12.8	11.5	11.4	10.9
55–60	18.5	18.4	18.4	19.2	17.5	17.1	16.6

The figures show that the death-rate declined very much
more quickly in the years of high unemployment than in the
years of lesser unemployment.

Although undoubtedly some factors bias health statistics
in times of depression so as to indicate a greater degree of good
health than actually prevails, death statistics confirm the
fact that general health conditions do indeed improve during
times of crisis and depression because the worker is less exposed
to injurious working conditions.

.   .   .   .   .   .

Many more factors contribute to the moulding of labour
conditions such as migrations of industry, structural changes
in the composition of industry, the introduction of vacations,
and of new means of transport (the bicycle, the under-
ground, railroads, etc.), increases or decreases of women's
employment, the possibility or impossibility to supplement
wages by gardening, etc.

They all help to improve or worsen labour conditions ;
they all either enable employers to increase the intensity
of work or make it necessary for them to find relief measures
for keeping intensity at the high level reached.

The effect of many of them on labour conditions cannot
be measured accurately at present. Some of them cannot at
all be dealt with statistically. Of some of them the effects
are not known at all. Some affect labour conditions in both
ways, at once improving them and making them worse.

* Cf., *Statistisches Jahrbuch für das Deutsche Reich*, 1933 and 1935.

They all, however, need a much more thorough investigation as to their importance to the worker, and, of course, none of them should be forgotten if one wants to investigate labour conditions as thoroughly as possible.

It is advisable to start an investigation of labour conditions with an investigation of real wages.

Real wages should then be corrected according to changes in short-time and unemployment, and according to changes in taxation and social insurance dues.

Then strike costs, trade union dues, and wage losses through accidents and sickness should be computed. On the other side, the benefits from social insurance systems must be deducted from wage losses.

A thorough investigation of the changes of the commodities the worker buys comes next ; they include rooms, textiles, food, etc.

Health conditions irrespective of wage losses through time lost because of illness have then to be examined.

After an evaluation of these and other factors bearing on absolute labour conditions relative wages should be computed.

In all these investigations of long-range changes of labour conditions the fact that labour conditions deteriorate in the long run, should not take up much of our space ; that is a fact which should be stated at the beginning. The important thing to be found out is the method and the way in which labour conditions deteriorate, the change in the methods the employers use to get as high profits as possible, the consequences of the different methods upon the life of the worker, and finally, the line the worker should take under present conditions in his efforts to secure labour conditions worsening at a less rapid pace.

IV. LABOUR AND LABOUR CONDITIONS

If labour conditions are, in the long run, bound to deteriorate—what is the justification of all the efforts of labour to improve labour conditions ? Are those right who argue : " Labour must try to overthrow the capitalist government and, in order to succeed, labour must fight whenever it can to prepare for the final battle ; but it is not only useless but dangerous to fight, for example, in Parliament, to fight for social insurance, to fight for influential positions within the capitalist state, for it fosters illusions as to the possibility of improving the status of labour within capitalist society " ?

This line of argument is, as far as the second part of the argument is concerned, absolutely wrong and counter to all the experience of labour itself. True, labour cannot improve labour conditions in the long run within capitalist society. But it can slow up considerably the pace of deterioration. Labour conditions are by no means physically and morally as bad as possible. If this were the case there would be no room for labour conditions to deteriorate still further. If labour conditions had reached the minimum point of existence, or gone below this point, capitalist society could not continue to exist ; for, while labour can live without capitalists, while a labour society can very well exist though former capitalists starve, yet capitalist society cannot live without labour, and without a labour force still able to do an increasing amount of most intensive work.

Therefore, labour has every reason to fight against the continuous process of further deterioration of labour conditions. Labour can, by means of good party and trade union organizations, slow up substantially the process of deterioration. Labour can, by able strategy, force the employers to apply certain alleviating means which give labour a better position, such as, for instance, social insurance.

While the decisive contest between labour and capital is for supremacy, the thousands of skirmishes for improving labour conditions within the capitalist state try to turn to as much account as possible a battle doomed to be lost within present-day society (for labour conditions are bound to deteriorate). And the importance of this tactical fight must by no means be underestimated. For the result of each of these thousands of skirmishes helps to determine labour conditions as long as capitalist society exists. While the decisive battle is fought for and against the very existence of capitalist society the thousands of skirmishes are concerned with the degree of deterioration of labour conditions within capitalist society.

Only those who keep both of these aims in mind, only

those who recognize their true values and respective importance are real labour leaders, are real labour strategists.
Neglect of any one of them must necessarily handicap
labour, must necessarily lead to superfluous sacrifices, is
necessarily disadvantageous, dangerous and injurious to
labour in its fight against capitalism.

Chapter II

LABOUR CONDITIONS IN ENGLAND

In investigating labour conditions in England we must keep in mind that we are not dealing with a capitalist organism as a whole but only with a section. We deal only with England, and not with English capitalist society, which also comprises India and Canada and Australia, etc. There is no reason, therefore, to assume that labour conditions in England proper had the tendency to deteriorate continuously as they did in English capitalist society as a whole. Our investigation of labour conditions in England therefore, has a twofold scope : firstly, to find out whether and when labour conditions did deteriorate, and secondly, how they changed, whether slowly or quickly, whether through decreases or increases of real wages, through the introduction of social insurance systems, through the deterioration or improvement of housing conditions, etc.

The statistical material available or procurable for gauging labour conditions in England during the nineteenth and twentieth centuries is poor as, indeed, it is for all other countries. But though it is poor, it is comparatively better than for most other countries. This holds especially true of wage statistics. We begin our investigation of labour conditions, therefore, with a survey of wages in England (see p. 70). The first of the wage tables gives the wages year by year, the second gives the wages for individual industries at different periods, and the third, which is the most instructive table, gives the wages by business-cycle averages.

If wage averages are given at all they generally are given as purely arbitrary averages, five-yearly or ten-yearly, or any other mechanical average. In a ten-year average there may be included the low points of two crises or the high points of two phases of prosperity, and thus the average may be " loaded " this way or that. But if we choose as average a varying number of years, determined by the

duration of the business-cycle, we can avoid that one
average contains, for example, twice, wages pulled down by
heavy unemployment at the low point of two crises, while
the next average contains not a single year of deep crisis.*

. . . . . .

If we look first at Table III it seems that we can distinguish three periods—the twenties and the first years of
the thirties of the nineteenth century, the rest of the nineteenth century, and the twentieth century. During the first
period real wages seem to have declined slightly ; during
the second period they seem to have increased considerably,
and during the third period they seem to have declined
again. Of the total of 115 years under review real wages
seem to have increased for about two-thirds of the time.

This, however, is not really the case. For the period
up to 1850 we only have data for gross real wages, that is
wage data not taking into account, for instance, wage losses
through unemployment. The small increase, for example,
from 1833–42 to 1843–49 would be more than wiped out if
we could include data on unemployment, especially in 1847
and 1848 ; for in these years unemployment reached unprecedented heights which probably were reached again only
in the last crisis. Furthermore, the increase of gross real
wages from 1827–32 to 1833–42 is due to the fact that we
chiefly had wage data for a number of skilled trades, and
even there only for grown-up workers. If we could take
into account the enormous increase in the proportion of
women and of children, especially of the latter, employed at
wages which, in the case of children, often did not amount
to a shilling per week, our table would undoubtedly show
not an increase, but rather a decrease of real wages.

Taking into account unemployment and women's and
children's wages, one may safely say that net real wages
declined up to the middle of the last century.

From the middle of the century up to the end net real
wages of workers employed by English capitalism in England

* I have used the cyclical average for quite a number of computations
in recent books. Professor Bowley informed me that he himself had
used this method of averaging, but that he never had published such
averages though he approves of them.

probably have increased from business-cycle to business-cycle. However, before we begin to look more closely at this increase of real wages it is opportune to give some account of labour conditions in the 'forties.

At this time, the working-day was probably longer than at any other time in English history. It had increased during the whole first third of the century, and in the following years a constantly growing number of workers had to work up to sixteen and eighteen hours per day. The number of women and children employed increased both absolutely and relatively. It was by no means rare to find the man unemployed at home, while his wife and children were in the factory. If the man was also employed, the babies were drugged to keep them quiet while the mother was working. The drugs had such appealing names as Infant's Preservative and Mother's Blessing. As soon as the children could work, which often meant as soon as they had reached the ripe age of three or four years, they were carried to the factory to start earning their own living. One of these children later on described its experiences as follows :

" Children were sent to work in factories so young that one of our informants says he was carried on his father's back to Rand's mill, where there was a cistern of cold water specially kept for dipping sleepy children in to keep them awake. As a consequence deformity and spinal weakness too frequently prevailed."*

In 1841, the member for Birmingham, Mr. Scholefield, moved in the House of Commons :

" That the extreme sufferings of the industrial classes from want of employment, low wages, and the high prices of provisions, render it the imperative duty of Parliament to devise means for the alleviation of the great misery which now prevails in the manufacturing districts of the country."

But the House was so little interested in this matter that it was counted out during the discussion.

The best description of labour conditions at this time is that by Engels in his book, *The Condition of the Working Class*

* Cf., W. Cudworth, *Condition of the Industrial Classes of Bradford and District.*

in England in 1844. From this study as well as from government reports and most other sources dealing with labour conditions, it is obvious that labour had reached the limits of misery and endurance. The working-day could not be lengthened any more, wages could not be lowered any more, the health of the working class could not be undermined any more, without (in many cases) leading to a complete cessation of work.

. . . .

On the other hand, the capitalist class, of course, wanted to continue to exploit English labour, wanted to continue the accumulation of capital, and to keep the factories producing more and more commodities. Since further exploitation and absorption of surplus value through a lengthening of the working-day was impossible, and since wages had gone down below the minimum of subsistence level, the only possibility of augmenting the surplus value derived from employing labour was to increase the intensity of work per hour. An increase of intensity of work per hour was possible, however, only by feeding the workers better, so that they were physically able to work at greater speed. This, however, necessitated a rise in purchasing power. This required, furthermore, increasing the proportion of grown-up workers. And this in its turn demanded the reorganization of the production process.

English capitalism did not see this quite clearly from the very beginning. English capitalism did not choose this way of exploiting the workers and increasing the surplus value fully conscious of what it was doing. But in the course of a comparatively few years, more and more employers began to shorten the hours of work, began to increase the purchasing power of the worker, and began to employ relatively more grown-up workers instead of children.

If we look at the whole development of labour conditions in England during the 'fifties and following years from this point of view, it becomes clear why the English capitalist suddenly turned socially minded, why, suddenly, factory inspectors had the power to say and to do things which, in the first half of the century, and even more so in the first third, would have been impossible. The whole structure of English industrial production changed its aspect because the way of appropriating surplus value had changed. Increasing the intensity of work per hour and relinquishing the increase of intensity of work per day through lengthening the working-day, became the " fashion " among English capitalists to be followed later on by those of other countries.

In this way, the fact and the significance of a half-century of increasing real wages and decreasing hours of work are easily explained. Both movements, that of real wages and that of hours of work, are nothing else than the result of the application of certain means of alleviating the effects of the "new method" of exploitation, of extracting surplus value chiefly through the increase of the intensity of work per hour.

Although this is the chief reason for the change in policy of the capitalist class, many other factors contributed to facilitate and quicken this change. The capitalists thought it advantageous—and rightly so—to gain the support of organized labour in its culminating struggle with landed property. Labour at the end of the 'forties was, if not lastingly at least strongly organized, and of considerable political influence in certain periods of crisis. The " great Liberal Party " did not mind at all having labour turned into its tail to lash out with, if need be, against the still stubbornly struggling landed aristocracy.

The years following the 'forties were also years of rapidly growing investments in English colonies and other countries.

Between 1853 and 1864 about £40,000,000 were subscribed for Indian railways. In 1857 about £80,000,000 of American railroad stock were held in England. Between 1852 and 1858 about $60,000,000 were required for building railroads and canals in Canada, and the bulk of this money came from England. In France, in each of the six years after 1851 almost £30,000,000 were spent upon railway construction. A large part of the capital outlay came from England, and at the construction of the Paris and Rouen railway, among 10,000 workers employed upwards of 4,000 were English.[*]

This enormous capital investment in foreign countries undoubtedly brought great amounts of extra profits of which a small part was given to the English working class. And

* Cf., C. K. Hobson, *The Export of Capital.*

with increasing extra profits the English capitalist class could become " larger and larger-minded " in handling the exploitation of the English worker.

Looking back over the more than forty years from 1844 to 1885 Engels writes in the *London Commonweal* :

" . . . And the condition of the working class during this period ? There was temporary improvement even for the great mass. . . . A permanent improvement can be recognized for two ' protected ' sections only of the working class. Firstly, the factory hands. . . . They are undoubtedly better off than before 1848. . . . Secondly, the great Trades Unions. . . .

" But as to the great mass of working people, the state of misery and insecurity in which they live now is as low as ever, if not lower. . . .

" The truth is this : during the period of England's industrial monopoly the English working class have, to a certain extent, shared in the benefits of the monopoly. These benefits were very unequally parcelled out amongst them ; the privileged minority pocketed most, but even the great mass had, at least, a temporary share now and then."

These remarks of Engels refer to the period from before 1848 to the end of the 'sixties. From the end of the 'forties to the end of the 'sixties real wages in England increased according to our table—1900 equals 100—from 52 (1843–9) to 63 (1859–68). A relatively small part of this increase was due to the changing structure of industry (e.g., from agriculture to industry, or from textiles to iron and steel). Since, at the same time, many other factors influencing labour conditions, such as health conditions within the factories or transport conditions from the home to the factory or the length of the working-day had improved, it may be quite possible that, even taking into account the increased intensity of work, labour conditions in England proper improved somewhat during the fifties and sixties of the last century.

For the first fifty years under review we thus arrive at the following conclusion. During the years from 1820 to 1850 labour conditions in England have deteriorated. At the end of the 'forties they were undoubtedly worse than at the beginning of the 'twenties. During the years from 1850 to 1870 labour conditions very probably improved—at the expense of labour employed by English capital outside England. Whether at the end of the 'sixties they were appreciably better than at the beginning of the 'twenties, that is whether they improved considerably more than they had deteriorated before, is doubtful. The material available does not permit us to form any definite opinion. That the worker was better fed and better clothed is very probable. That this improvement compensated, or did more than that for the increased intensity of work may be possible. Hence it may be possible that labour conditions in England were better absolutely in 1870 as compared with 1820—at the expense of labour employed by English capital abroad.

Looking upon the individual industries and trades one notices, of course, great differences. In the period from 1850 to 1870 labour conditions in agriculture, very probably, did not improve but deteriorated. Nor did any improvement take place in the printing industry. Also in the coal industry one probably cannot find any improvement in labour conditions. In other industries like the textile industry, undoubtedly, labour conditions were better at the end of the 'sixties than at the end of the 'forties, and that not only because of the shift from children to grown-up workers.

.   .   .   .   .   .

From the end of the 'sixties to the end of the 'eighties real wages continued to increase. They rose—1900 equals 100— from 63 (1859–68) to 91 (1887–95). About one-third of this increase is due to shifts from lower-paying industries to higher-paying industries, that is : to the changing structure of English economic society. More and more comparatively low-paying work is done by labour employed by English capital outside of England. In factories, situated in England, a constantly increasing proportion of work is done by skilled and comparatively higher-paid workers. Agriculture and textiles lose in relative importance.

For the years 1859–68 to 1887–95 we find an average yearly increase of real wages only slightly smaller than for the years 1843–9 to 1859–68—if we investigate only the wage of the worker staying for the whole time within the same industry. However, we must realize that other factors influencing labour conditions improved very much less from 1859–68 to 1887–95 than during the preceding period, that the great improvement in general health conditions and by far the greater part of the shortening of hours took place from the end of the 'forties to the end of the 'sixties, and that comparatively little improvement as regards working-time and health conditions took place in the 'seventies and 'eighties. We must keep in mind too, that the intensity of work was increased considerably, and that housing conditions during the 'seventies and 'eighties not only did not improve, but that an increasing number of workers were driven to live in terribly congested areas. It seems probable, therefore, that labour conditions as a whole during the 'seventies and 'eighties did not improve, but remained stationary, or even may have deteriorated.

Real wages undoubtedly did increase during this period. But labour conditions did not improve. Some of the most terrible adverse effects upon labour conditions we find caused by the congestion in the great cities. This congestion destroyed any vestige of home life for the worker which the shortening of hours may have permitted. At the same time, the living conditions within the cities deteriorated in so far as the workers became more and more segregated. If, about 1820, a worker was unemployed he lived in the larger factory villages and even in the great cities together with other workers, craftsmen, and small tradesmen who had employment or their small business, and could help him. If, in 1870, a worker became unemployed, he had to move to poorer and poorer quarters, to those city districts where the down-and-outs lived, and where nobody could help the other because they were all equally badly off. In this way, for example, the living conditions of the unemployed, even if he had the same amount of money saved, or even if he received the same amount of bread or soup from a charitable organization as fifty years ago, were very much worse in 1870 than they were in 1820.

Thus, we may safely conclude that the living conditions of the unemployed undoubtedly deteriorated very much during the nineteenth century, especially during the second half.

Among the individual industries an outstanding example,

during the 'seventies and 'eighties, of an industry with increasingly unfavourable labour conditions, especially also as far as wages relative to other industries are concerned, was the woollen and worsted industry. The coal industry too shows a very unfavourable development of labour conditions. Puddling also was a trade in which labour conditions deteriorated. In agriculture very little, if any, improvement took place.

Compared with the preceding period of twenty years or so, one may say, perhaps, that the number of industries and trades which showed a deterioration of labour conditions increased, and that the extent of deterioration was very much higher than it was in the fewer industries during the preceding phase. On the other hand, the improvement which took place in a smaller number of industries than during the preceding years, was undoubtedly less significant than in the greater number of industries for which during the 'fifties and 'sixties an improvement of labour conditions could be reported.

If we said that labour conditions were about the same at the end of the 'eighties as at the end of the 'sixties one must by no means conclude that this judgment about a general average holds true for the individual industries. For in many of them the suffering of the workers had increased very much during this period.

That during the nineties of the last century no improvement of labour conditions took place is quite obvious from the report on the physical deterioration of the working class which we have discussed more extensively already above.*

For the nineteenth century we thus can conclude as follows :

1820 to 1850 : deterioration of labour conditions, probably quite considerable.

1850 to 1870 : improvement of labour conditions, at the expense of workers employed by English capital outside of England. Possibly labour conditions at the end of the 'sixties were, in an absolute sense, better than at the beginning of the 'twenties.

1870 to 1900 : during the whole of this period labour conditions in general did not improve, but very probably

* See pp. 34–36 of this book.

were about the same, or possibly somewhat worse, at the end of the 'nineties as compared with the end of the 'sixties at the expense of increased exploitation of workers outside of England employed by English capital.

.   .   .   .   .   .

Before we follow the trend of labour conditions into the twentieth century, it is necessary to say a few words about the standard of living at the close of the nineteenth century. A great amount of evidence is available to give some kind of picture of labour conditions about this time. For at the beginning of the 'nineties a Royal Commission on Labour took evidence from a great number of men concerning a great many factors influencing labour conditions in all the important trades which employ labour. Among the great number of witnesses we will quote only two : Sidney Webb and Sir R. Giffen. Both are recognized authorities on their subject, and both are of the opinion that labour conditions can improve and do improve under the capitalist system in the long run, either as Sir R. Giffen thinks by slow reform or as Sidney Webb proposes by more far-reaching and quicker reforms. Both are opposed to the Marxist opinion that labour conditions do not improve within a capitalist organism in the long run.

When asked by Tom Mann, a member of the Labour Commission :*

" . . . So that we are to understand from that whilst I think you have admitted that the standard of the wage-earners is higher than it was, they have not absorbed the full value of their increased product."

Sidney Webb answered :

" They have not received an equivalent share of the increase in productivity which has resulted ; and many large classes have not had their standard of life raised at all."

The first part of the answer refers to the movement of the relative position of the worker, a problem we shall deal with later on. The second part of the answer is : the standard

* *Fourth Report of the Royal Commission of Labour*, London, 1893. " Minutes of Evidence taken before the Royal Commission on Labour, Sitting as a Whole," p. 293.

of life of the wage earners is higher than it was in former times (a statement with which we agree since by former times is meant the 'forties), but many large groups of the working class did not have their standard of life raised at all.

But looking at this higher average standard of life prevailing in the 'nineties as compared with the 'forties, we find that this higher standard nevertheless meant for a great number of workers a standard of terrible poverty.

When asked by the Duke of Devonshire :*

" Your tables show, I think, that a very large proportion of the working class of the country are earning very low wages ? "

Sir R. Giffen answered :

" Yes ; I think that really is the important impression which one gets, that although you have three-fourths of the working classes, that is, of the men, earning between 50 l. and 60 l. per annum and upwards, yet you have 25 per cent, or something like that, below the line of 20s. per week, and that is really below the line that one would consider expedient for a minimum subsistence."

25 per cent of the working class below the line of the minimum of subsistence—and that not in the hungry 'forties but in the 'nineties when labour conditions were about as good, or only very little worse than at the end of the 'sixties, probably the peak of the labour conditions in the history of English capitalism.

.   .   .   .

In the above-mentioned article Engels closed his survey of the last forty years with some remarks about the future economic development in England :

" . . . the manufacturing monopoly of England is the pivot of the present social system of England. . . . With the breakdown of that monopoly, the English working class will lose that privileged position [of living partly at the expense of workers employed by English capital abroad, J.K.] ; it will find itself generally—the privileged and leading minority not excepted—on a level with its fellow-workers abroad."

This prophesy began very soon to become true. Since 1895–1903 real wages in England have declined from

* l.c., p. 475.

F

business-cycle to business-cycle. The intensity of work has risen enormously. The introduction of health insurance was a not very effective palliative against the neglect of housing conditions in the cities. The introduction of unemployment insurance did not offset the wage losses through increased unemployment. It is true that the cinema and the radio have done very much to enliven the worker's life, but on the other side they have helped to sidetrack him often from his interest in politics. It is true that during recent years housing conditions have improved, sometimes considerably, but at the expense of other things which the worker, with the increased rent in better houses, cannot afford any more. It is true that unemployment insurance has removed some of the insecurity in the worker's life, but the non-financial ill-effects of unemployment upon the worker's life have, through the great length of the unemployment periods, become so disastrously important that they often more than make up for the money the worker gets in addition to the charity he would have received before unemployment insurance was introduced.

If we look at the individual industries we can observe that the difference of the development has increased very much. There are industries in which labour conditions have grown worse very much more quickly and very much more than the average of industry as a whole. The difference in the development of the coal industry, of textiles, and of shipbuilding on the one side, and of agriculture, of building and of the electrical industry on the other side, has been very great indeed during the twentieth century. And the difference between the electrical industry in which labour conditions probably improved (and are often better than in many other industries at the peak of their prosperity whenever it was) and of agriculture, where labour conditions during the twentieth century probably have not grown worse but have remained stable at the incredibly low standard reached during the nineteenth century, is often unbelievable.

·   ·   ·   ·   ·   ·

Looking back over the development of labour conditions during the last 115 years, we find only a very short period of about twenty years (1850 to 1870) during which labour conditions in England proper really did improve absolutely. During the following thirty years (1870 to 1900) it is not certain whether labour conditions deteriorated or remained stable. During the sixty-five years, 1820 to 1850 and 1900 to 1935, labour conditions undoubtedly did deteriorate.

The years of improving or stable labour conditions were years during which English capitalists made enormous extra profits through employing labour outside of England, partly in the colonies and partly in other countries, whether Continental or American. Some extra profits were made also in the years before 1850, and very high extra profits were made, of course, also during the twentieth century. But the rate of extra profits has declined during the last forty years, and as Engels expected, this decline of the rate of profits (not of the mass which probably has increased still for quite a time, while the rate already declined) has been felt severely by the workers of England proper.

If one would be able to compute, for example, Empire wages, or better still, an average wage of all workers employed by English capital wherever it is employing workers, the picture of the development of the absolute conditions of " English " labour would be a very different one. There would be a rapid decline and deterioration of the absolute standard of living during the whole of the nineteenth century. Assuming only that real wages (not labour conditions, of course !) in India during the last sixty years had risen by, for example, 50 per cent, and that the number of Indian workers employed by English capital had risen fifty times (which would be no exaggeration) it is easily conceivable that the addition of so many very low-paid workers, even if their real wages had increased by 50 per cent, would pull down the average wage of Indian and English workers constantly and considerably, because of the increasing weight of the Indian workers among the whole of the workers employed by English capitalism.

If we add to the millions of Indian workers Chinese workers employed in English mines in China, the African natives working in South Africa, the Italians working in Argentine meat-slaughtering houses, and all the other millions of coloured or white wage earners employed by English capital everywhere in the world—and if we realize how very much this number has increased during the last century, then every doubt one may have must be dispelled, and it must seem an obvious commonplace that labour conditions under English capitalism have not improved but deteriorated, that the average standard of living of the worker employed by English capital must have declined considerably during the last and the present century.

If we take into account all these considerations, if we remember what a great part of mankind is working under English capitalism, then one will realize also that our study of the development of labour conditions in England proper is not only a purely sectional study, but that it comprises only a comparatively small section of the workers employed by English capitalism. And even this small section of the whole working class employed by English capitalism, this small section of privileged workers—for the whole of the English working class is privileged in a certain sense as compared with other workers employed by English capital abroad—had only twenty years during which their labour conditions beyond doubt improved!

. . . .

While the absolute living conditions of the English worker had improved for about twenty years at the expense of workers employed abroad by English capital, and while they have remained about stable for perhaps thirty years more, or declined relatively little during this period, the relative position of the English worker has deteriorated continuously and very considerably.

The relative position of the English worker is determined by the relation of real wages to the national product per consumer in England. Unfortunately, English production statistics are of a very low standard. It was a German scholar who recently constructed an index of industrial production for England. An index of agricultural production is non-existent, and the computation of a national product, taking into account exports and imports, is, with the material available, a piece of research work requiring a very considerable amount of time. Nobody in England was interested enough in this problem to construct an index of the national product of England, that is an index of industrial and agricultural production taking into account changes in exports and imports.

Since already the real wage data available are, of course, only rough approximations to an index of the standard of living, and since we relate this index of real wages to an index of industrial production per consumer only, our index of relative wages is only indicative of the tendency of the movement, and errors of several per cent are not only probable, but it would be only by accident if they did not occur.

The exclusion of agricultural production is not so serious an omission as it would be, for example, in dealing with Germany, since agricultural production already in 1859, when our index of relative wages begins, was very small. But, on the whole, only the fact that the trend of relative wages, their downward movement, is such a decided one, makes it permissible to publish these computations.

If we look at Table IV (see p. 81) we find that from 1859–68 to 1924–32 relative wages have declined by about 40 per cent. If we take into account a great number of factors which we did not include into our real wage index and which undoubtedly would have smoothed their upward trend and increased their downward trend, the decline of relative wages would have seemed a greater one. On the other hand the exclusion of agriculture probably hastens the downward trend of relative wages because national production as a whole probably did increase at a smaller pace than industrial production only. Weighting both sides, the one tending to hasten the decline of relative wages and the other tending to slow up the decline, one probably may be right in saying that they might cancel each other in the long run. One might incline perhaps to the opinion that the pace of the decline of relative wages as indicated in our table probably does, on the whole, not exaggerate nor minimize the actual movement of relative wages.

The pace of relative deterioration of labour conditions has slowed up in the course of time. With increasing absolute deterioration of labour conditions relative labour conditions have deteriorated less quickly. In the beginning of the second half of the nineteenth century, when English capitalism was still comparatively young and still in the flower of its strength, when industrial production increased at a rate not to be approached again, in that period the relative position of the worker declined rapidly. This holds true too —reliable figures, however, are not available—of the first half of the nineteenth century. In the last twenty years of the nineteenth century, however, the pace began to slacken considerably, and has increased only in post-War years.

The table of relative wages shows clearly that no " uplifting of the working class " has taken place. On the contrary the working class in England has been let down continuously, and in the course of time the gap between the ruling class and the working class has been widened more and more. Even in those years, or rather just in those years during which labour conditions in England proper improved a little absolutely, the abyss between the " two nations " has grown in size at an unprecedented rate.

To-day the English ruling class is very much richer than it ever was, absolutely and relatively, while the working class is worse off absolutely than at the end of the last century, and relatively worse off than ever in its history. The relative position of the worker 100 years ago undoubtedly was a better one than to-day, the abyss between the ruling class and the working class was, undoubtedly, very much smaller 100 years ago than to-day.

TABLE I

WAGES IN THE UNITED KINGDOM
(1900 = 100)

Year	Gross Money Wages*	Net Money Wages†	Net Real Wages per Full-Time Week§	Net Real Wages per Unemployed and Employed Worker	Cost of Living
1820	55	—	37	—	150
1821	55	—	47	—	117
1822	54	—	46	—	117
1823	52	—	41	—	127
1824	54	—	42	—	130
1825	54	—	43	—	127
1826	53	—	46	—	117
1827	53	—	45	—	117
1828	53	—	45	—	117
1829	53	—	40	—	130
1830	52	—	40	—	130
1831	51	—	42	—	124
1832	52	—	42	—	124
1833	52	—	48	—	109
1834	53	—	51	—	104
1835	52	—	57	—	91
1836	53	—	51	—	104
1837	53	—	49	—	109
1838	54	—	45	—	119
1839	54	—	47	—	117
1840	55	—	47	—	118
1841	54	—	49	—	111
1842	54	—	47	—	114
1843	54	—	54	—	99
1844	54	—	52	—	104
1845	55	—	54	—	101
1846	57	—	53	—	108
1847	57	—	45	—	127
1848	55	—	50	—	109
1849	53	—	53	—	100
1850	56	55	60	59	94
1851	56	55	61	60	92
1852	56	54	61	59	92
1853	62	62	62	63	99
1854	64	64	57	57	112

TABLE I—continued

Year	Gross Money Wages*	Net Money Wages†	Net Real Wages per Full-Time Week§	Net Real Wages per Unemployed and Employed Worker	Cost of Living
1855	65	63	56	55	115
1856	65	64	57	56	115
1857	62	60	57	55	110
1858	62	56	60	55	102
1859	62	62	62	61	101
1860	64	64	61	62	105
1861	64	62	59	58	108
1862	65	61	62	58	105
1863	66	64	64	62	102
1864	69	70	68	69	101
1865	71	71	69	69	103
1866	74	73	68	68	109
1867	73	70	64	61	114
1868	73	69	65	61	112
1869	73	70	67	64	109
1870	75	74	69	68	109
1871	77	78	71	72	109
1872	82	83	71	73	114
1873	87	88	75	76	116
1874	87	88	77	78	113
1875	86	87	79	79	109
1876	85	85	79	79	108
1877	85	83	77	76	110
1878	83	79	76	73	108
1879	82	75	79	72	103
1880	82	80	77	75	106
1881	82	82	78	78	105
1882	82	83	78	78	106
1883	83	84	80	81	104
1884	84	80	82	78	102
1885	84	78	93	87	90
1886	83	77	86	79	96
1887	84	79	89	84	94
1888	85	83	90	88	94
1889	87	88	90	91	97
1890	91	92	94	95	97
1891	91	91	93	93	98
1892	90	88	93	90	98
1893	93	86	97	90	96

TABLE I—*continued*

Year	Gross Money Wages*	Net Money Wages†	Net Real Wages per Full-Time Week§	Net Real Wages per Unemployed and Employed Worker	Cost of Living
1894	90	87	96	92	94
1895	90	88	98	95	93
1896	91	91	99	99	92
1897	93	92	98	98	94
1898	94	94	98	98	96
1899	96	97	101	102	95
1900	100	100	100	100	100
1901	99	98	107	106	93
1902	98	96	98	97	100
1903	97	95	97	95	101
1904	97	93	96	93	101
1905	97	95	96	94	101
1906	99	98	98	97	101
1907	102	101	99	97	104
1908	102	96	97	92	105
1909	100	95	96	90	105
1910	101	98	95	93	106
1911	101	101	95	94	107
1912	104	101	93	92	110
1913	107	106	95	95	111
1914	108	105	97	96	110
1924	190	178	91	90	198
1925	191	180	93	93	194
1926	192	179	93	91	196
1927	188	178	97	96	185
1928	186	175	96	95	184
1929	185	174	96	95	183
1930	184	160	103	94	170
1931	179	152	104	94	162
1932	177	150	106	96	157
1933	176	153	106	97	157
1934	177	158	107	100	158
1935	179	164	106	102	161

* Without taking into account wage losses and gains through short-time, unemployment, taxes, social insurance payments, social insurance benefits etc.

† Taking into account wage losses through unemployment (1850 to 1935) and social insurance payments (1912 to 1935) and unemployment insurance benefits (1924 to 1935).

§ Taking into account social insurance payments.

TABLE II

GROSS MONEY WAGES BY INDUSTRIES IN THE
UNITED KINGDOM
(1850 = 100)

Trade	1820	1825	1830	1835	1840	1845	1850
Agriculture	103	90	93	91	95	97	100
Building	98	98	91	91	98	98	100
Shipbuilding and Engineering ..	97	97	96	97	103	103	100
Coal	—	—	—	—	103	90	100
Cotton	102	101	87	90	95	105	100
Printing	94	94	94	94	100	100	100
Average	99	96	92	93	98	98	100

Trade	(1900 = 100) 1850	1855	1860	1866	1871	1874
Agriculture*						
I.	64	76	76	80	84	94
II.	50	63	60	60	71	85
III.	60	61	67	71	77	80
Building	58	63	68	75	77	84
Printing	81	81	81	82	86	91
Shipbuilding	64	71	68	77	78	85
Engineering	67	74	73	77	80	87
Coal	62	87	71	93	74	100
Puddling	66	89	66	84	78	103
Cotton	54	59	67	74	80	84
Wool and Worsted† ..	67	75	82	87	90	100
Worsted‡	72	73	82	92	104	127
Gas	67	68	70	73	80	86
Furniture	66	68	71	78	81	91
Average	56	65	64	74	77	87

Trade	(1900 = 100) 1880	1886	1891	1896	1900
Agriculture*					
I.	92	90	93	93	100
II.	85	87	91	95	100
III.	86	90	93	97	100
Building	87	87	91	95	100
Printing	94	94	98	99	100

TABLE II—*continued*

Trade					1880	1886	1891	1896	1900
Shipbuilding	..	..	..	..	82	82	95	94	100
Engineering	..	..	..	..	82	84	93	96	100
Coal	..	..	..	..	67	67	93	81	100
Puddling	..	..	..	..	81	64	72	65	100
Cotton	..	..	..	..	82	86	91	95	100
Wool and Worsted†	..	..	..		103	92	94	96	100
Worsted‡	..	..	..	..	97	96	96	98	100
Gas	..	..	..	..	87	87	96	97	100
Furniture	..	..	..	..	92	91	94	95	100
Average	..	..	..	..	82	83	91	91	100

Trade		1900	1905	1910	1914	1924	1930	1934
Agriculture	..	100	103	105	114	177	194	189
Building	..	100	100	100	108	198	191	179
Engineering	..	100	100	102	107	171	173	168
Coal	..	100	81	90	99	132	114	112
Textiles	..	100	103	107	112	188	173	160
Average	..	100	97	101	108	190	184	177

* I = England and Wales ; II = Scotland ; III = Ireland.
† Huddersfield only.
‡ Bradford only.

TABLE III

NET REAL WAGES IN THE UNITED KINGDOM*

(Cyclical Averages, 1900 = 100)

Cycle		Index
1820–6	..	43
1827–32	..	42
1833–42	..	49
1843–9	..	52
1849–58	..	57
1859–68	..	63
1869–79	..	74
1880–6	..	80
1887–95	..	91
1895–1903	..	99
1904–8	..	95
1909–14	..	93
1924–32	..	93

* 1820–50 gross real wages per full-time week, 1850–1932 taking unemployment into account, 1912–32 taking social insurance payments into account, 1924–32 taking unemployment insurance payments and benefits into account.

SOURCES AND REMARKS

The figure for 1924–32 would be 92, if one would take into account trade union dues, while the figures for the preceding cycles would not be changed through the deduction of trade union dues. The sources from which the data of the preceding three tables are computed are :

Wages, 1820 *to* 1850. Computed on the basis of the wage figures given by A. L. Bowley and H. G. Wood in their studies " The Statistics of Wages in the United Kingdom during the last Hundred Years," *Journal of the Royal Statistical Society,* 1899 to 1910 ; on the basis of the wage figures given in *Returns of Wages, Published between* 1830 *and* 1886, London, 1887 ; and on the basis of the data given in Bowley *Wages in the United Kingdom in the Nineteenth Century,* London, 1900.

Wages, 1850 *to* 1900. Cf., Wood, " Real Wages and the Standard of Comfort since 1850," *Journal of the Royal Statistical Society,* 1909.

Wages, 1900 *to* 1914. Cf., *Abstract of Labour Statistics of the United Kingdom,* 1926.

Wages, 1914 *and* 1925. Computed on the basis of the data given in *Abstract of Labour Statistics, Ministry of Labour Gazette,* Bowley; " A new index number of Wages," Memorandum 28, *London and Cambridge Economist Service* ; and E. C. Ramsbottom, "The Course of Wage Rates in the United Kingdon, 1921–34," *Journal of the Royal Statistical Society.* Wages 1924 refer to December. Wages for building in Table II, 1924, refer to skilled workers only, the general average figures, however, pertain to unskilled labour as well and include for the year 1924 many more industries than are enumerated separately.

Wages, 1924 *to* 1935. Cf., E. C. Ramsbottom, " The Course of Wage Rates in the United Kingdom, 1921–34," *Journal of the Royal Statistical Society,* 1935, and *Ministry of Labour Gazette.* The average figures in Table II include many more industries than are given separately.

Cost of Living, 1820 *to* 1850. Computed on the basis of price data for bread, sugar, cheese, butter, bacon and tea, given in *Wholesale and Retail Prices in the United Kingdom in* 1902, *with Comparative Statistical Tables for a Series of Years,* London, 1903, and on the basis of data given by Porter in " On a Comparative Statement of Prices and Wages during the Years from 1842 to 1849," *Journal of the Statistical Society of London,* 1850.

Cost of Living, 1850 *to* 1900. We used the computations by Wood (" Real Wages, etc.", see above) and the figures given by Wood for the total increase of rents, while Wood himself takes into account only half the increase because, as he argues, rooms have improved too ; since Wood on the other side does not take into account deteriorations in textiles, etc., and since the difficulties of constructing a cost-of-living index cannot, if at all, be solved in such a rough one-sided way, we turned to the original figures which Wood has given for rents.

Cost of Living, 1900 *to* 1914. Computed on the basis of the figures given in the *Abstract of Labour Statistics* and assuming that rents increased up to 1904 bi-yearly by 0.1s., remained stable from 1905 to 1912, and increased again by 0.1s. in 1913 and 1914. *Cost of Living,* 1914 *to* 1935. We used the official cost-of-living index.

Unemployment. We used the figures of unemployment in trade unions from 1850 to 1924 and for the years from 1924 to 1934, the percentage of insured workpeople unemployed, cf., *Abstract of Labour Statistics.* Unemployment insurance benefits are estimated to be 40 per cent of the average wage losses suffered from unemployment during the years 1924–30 and 1934–35, and 35 per cent during the years 1931–33.

Social Insurance Payments. We estimated them at 1½ per cent for the years 1912–14, at 5 per cent for the years 1924–30, and at 6 per cent for the years 1931–35.

As compared with the requirements we listed for satisfying wage data in the first chapter of this book, these tables fall short of them in a great number of respects. The wage data are, for example, a mixture of wage rates and actual full-time wages. For some industries wage rates are the only data given, for other industries wage rates and actual wages are mixed, for some industries wage rates are given for a certain number of years and actual wages for another period. For some periods only a very limited number of wage data are available, especially for the years 1820 to 1850. A number of industries are not represented at all. Other industries are represented only by a limited number of occupations, mostly by skilled workers. The unemployment data for the nineteenth century pertain almost exclusively to skilled trades. The percentage of unemployment has a bias in so far as it is probably too low. No data on taxes are included. No data on time lost through strikes or stoppages, or accidents are included. Short-time has not been taken into account. Changes from male labour to female labour and child labour, and vice versa, have been taken into account, if at all, only for a limited number of years, and always insufficiently and without accurate basic material to work with. Wage data are overloaded with material from the big cities and the bigger establishments. To be brief : the whole wage material is from a theoretical point of view extremely unsatisfactory. It would be very wrong to draw any conclusion from these remarks as to an alleged inferior quality of, for example, the statistical work of the English pioneers of wage statistics. But it is perfectly correct to draw from these remarks the conclusion that English economic statisticians have done very little to progress on the path blazed with such immense diligence and painstaking labour by those first pioneers. This reproach is directed, of course, against the author of this study too. The data I have given above are by no means to be regarded as anything approaching a reliable index of wages, and the only table, though by no means accurate but at least probably not very erroneous, is Table III giving business-cycle averages, and thus compensating to some extent mistakes occurring in the year-to-year figures.

Although it may seem impossible, yet the index of cost of living is still more unreliable than the wage index. With the exception of the post-War years, our, as well as other authors' figures for rents, for example, are really only guesses —the term estimates would imply too much accuracy. Expenditures for illness is not taken into account. Expenditures for books, papers, magazines, pencils, pleasure, vacations, etc., is not included. The items included in the expense budget are often not bought at all by the workers, and if so, then very often in quantities quite different from those assumed.

English statisticians have computed excellent statistics of yields of government loans far back into the past. Is it really impossible to get them interested in the course of the living expenses of the great mass of the population?

The history of the study of the cost of living is exactly the same as that of the study of wages. After the pioneer work of Bowley and Wood, no serious effort has been made to continue and enlarge and improve their work.

But while for wages the government index which is computed currently is reliable in a certain way, as index namely of time rates mixed with a few piece rates, the English official cost-of-living index is not only very inadequate, but it is even worse than that of the United States and Germany.

Only great naïvety or else a good deal of optimism can induce one to use the cost-of-living index we have given as an accurate measure. And since the wage index neither is very reliable, no year-to-year real wage changes should be taken for an exact expression of what really has happened. The trend of the movement, on the other hand is indicated reliably. One should, however, keep in mind two things :

The cost-of-living index has a definite bias in showing the development of the cost of living as too favourable for the worker. If Wood argues that rooms have improved in the course of time, and therefore not the whole increase of rents should be included in the cost-of-living index, this argument does not seem logical. Because the worker always lives in the worst rooms available. If these rooms in the course of time become better, that is if the worst rooms in 1930 are better than the worst rooms in 1830, and if the rent is correspondingly higher, one cannot argue that, if such rooms as were inhabited by workers in 1830 would still exist to-day, the worker would get them to-day more cheaply than the rooms in which he actually lives. For the rooms of 1830 do not exist any more, and one cannot include prices of goods which are not to be had in the cost-of-living index. On the other hand, and these factors count very much in the worker's budget, the quality of clothing has undoubtedly become inferior to that of 30 and 100 years ago, and this deterioration of quality has lead to a more frequent renewal of the " wardrobe " of the worker. The shorter expectation of life of stockings and other clothing, has not been taken into account in the cost-of-living index. The increase of rents through the destruction of dilapidated buildings and the removal of the workers to newer and more expensive rooms is not taken into account for the post-War period. The increase in the direct taxes the worker pays does not find any expression in the cost-of-living index. The increasing amount of fare the worker has to pay in order to reach his working-place is not included in the cost-of-living index. These are only a few of the many items, which, in the course of time tend to increase absolutely or relatively the cost-of-living index, but which are not included in our index.

And in the same way as the cost-of-living index, the wage index has also a definite bias, an upward bias. The application of short-time has spread in the course of the last fifty years considerably. The omission of the growing losses through short-time tends to show a greater increase or smaller

decrease in money wages than actually took place. On the
other hand, the growing introduction of piece-rates instead
of time-rates tends to turn the wage index in the opposite
direction. The shift from skilled work to unskilled or half-
skilled work (and this factor is very important), lowers the
average wage level, a tendency which finds very inadequate
expression in our wage index. Furthermore, our wage index
excludes the income of salaried workers. Now the salaries
of clerks, of girls in department stores, etc., of the whole
group of salaried employees have gone up for the upper
10 per cent and have gone down considerably for the lower
90 per cent. While sixty years ago a salaried worker be-
longed socially and financially to an absolutely different
group than the worker, to-day many salaried workers are
lower paid than many wage-earners. The exclusion of salaried
workers contributes very much to distort the picture of the
development of living conditions of the working population.

Since, as we saw, both the index of cost of living as well
as the index of wages show a tendency to move in a direction
which give the impression of a more favourable development
of labour conditions than has actually taken place—one
might be justified in using our real wage index, arguing :
whatever its faults may be, if it goes down, one may be sure
that real wages have declined indeed, and if it goes up,
real wages surely have not gone up as much as the index
indicates, perhaps they have not gone up at all, perhaps they
may have even gone down.

TABLE IV

RELATIVE WAGES IN THE UNITED KINGDOM

(1900 = 100)

Cycles	Physical Volume of Industrial Production	Wholesale Prices	Retail Prices
1859–68	46	133	106
1869–79	62	129	110
1880–6	74	106	101
1887–95	83	91	96
1895–1903	97	89	96
1904–8	107	99	102
1909–14	117	108	108
1924–32	118	151	181

Cycles	Industrial per capita production, corrected according to relative price movements	Real Wages	Relative Wages
1859–68	51	63	124
1869–79	66	74	111
1880–6	83	80	96
1887–95	96	91	95
1895–1903	105	99	94
1904–8	104	95	91
1909–14	106	93	88
1924–32	119	93	78

Production. We used the index of industrial production computed by W. Hoffmann, *Weltwirtschaftliches Archiv,* 40. Band, September, 1934.

Wholesale Prices. We used the index of Sauerbeck and the Statist.

Retail Prices. Cf., p. 76 of this book.

Population. We used the official population statistics.

Real Wages. Cf., p. 76 of this book.

As we already remarked in the text the figures of relative wages are only rough approximations. We therefore have not given relative wages by years, but only by business-cycle averages. All the errors contained in the real wage index may have been multiplied by errors in the index of industrial per capita production. The only index really reliable is the index of population. The index of industrial production probably has a slight tendency to increase too quickly because of the omission of certain industries from this index. This slight tendency is changed into a definite bias through the omission of agricultural production. The wholesale price index suffers probably quite seriously from the omission of prices of finished products. Neither for England nor for any other country does a satisfactory wholesale price-index exist because prices of finished manufactured products are almost completely unknown and therefore, are not taken into account. About the shortcomings arising from substituting a cost-of-living index for a retail price-index and about the bad quality of the English cost-of-living index, we have spoken already.

As we have said already, the publication of our figures of relative wages is justified only because they show such a definite downward trend that there can be no doubt, notwith-

G

standing all the errors possible, that relative wages have declined very considerably in the course of the time reviewed here. We wish to add that we hope that our figures will soon fall into oblivion as a very crude first attempt, and that soon much more accurate figures will be published because the necessary research activity has been applied to this interesting and important subject.

CHAPTER III

LABOUR CONDITIONS IN GERMANY

LABOUR conditions in Germany developed in a way very similar to that in England. If one keeps in mind two facts : that industrialization started later and was slower in the beginning in Germany than in England, and that German imperialism did not develop with the same rapidity, until much later, and on a much smaller scale than in England, then almost all the differences in the development in England and Germany explain themselves very easily.

If we look at the development of wages (Table V), we observe at first a decline of real wages just as in England. But while in England this decline lasted only up to the end of the 'forties, in Germany real wages declined until far into the 'fifties. And while in England this decline was not so great that the former peak could not be reached quickly again, in Germany real wages did not attain the peak of 1830-39 before the end of the 'seventies.

The low point of real wages was reached in England at the end of the 'forties—taking losses through unemployment, etc., into account. At the end of the 'forties labour conditions in England had reached the end of one line of development. Real wages could not be lowered any further and hours of work could not be lengthened any more. The same situation we find in Germany about a decade later, around the middle of the 'fifties.

Not much is known of labour conditions in Germany about the middle of the century. While in England royal commissions and sincere friends of labour revealed the terrible plight of the English worker, German labour had not many such friends, and only few could give voice to their findings and opinions.

But the few data available indicate a degree of pauperization very similar to that in England, and in many respects worse. German labour probably was housed a little better than English labour and many of the evils of city congestion were not so pronounced in Germany, but other evils, especially those due to a greater degree of industrial feudalism, made labour conditions at least as difficult to endure as in England.

Already in 1828 Lieutenant-General von Horn drew the attention of the authorities to the fact that the extent of child labour and the conditions under which children had to work endangered the physical standing of the army, and that the physical deterioration of the population in the Rhenish industrial districts had reached such a point that the material from which recruits were drawn for the army, was growing worse and worse.

Another indication of the low standard of German labour is that English manufacturers again and again referred to the low standard of German labour, and to the competitive superiority of the German manufacturer because of these working conditions—if labour conditions in England should be improved. In answering these arguments of English employers, Macaulay could not refute the contention that labour conditions in Germany were even worse than in England, but answered as follows :*

" You try to frighten us by telling us that, in some German factories, the young work seventeen hours in the twenty-four, that they work so hard that among thousands there is not one who grows to such a stature that he can be admitted into the army ; and you ask whether, if we pass this bill, we can possibly hold our own against such competition as this ? Sir, I laugh at the thought of such competition. If we ever are forced to yield the foremost place among commercial nations, we shall yield it, not to a race of degenerate dwarfs, but to some people pre-eminently vigorous in body and in mind."

And yet, after the failure of the revolution of 1848, labour conditions had become still worse and during the following years labour conditions had grown so bad that only a race of degenerate dwarfs unable to produce or to defend the interests of the governing class in a war, could continue to live under them.

Just as in England it became absolutely necessary to

* *Speeches of Lord Macaulay, corrected by himself.* London, 1866. *Speech on the Ten-Hour Bill*, 22 May, 1846.

change the venue of exploitation. Just as in England, only about ten years later, it became necessary to increase real wages and to improve labour conditions in many other ways, if an increasing rate of surplus value was to be taken from the worker. Consequently real wages were raised, hours of work were shortened, child-labour was restricted—and as a result of these measures the intensity of work could be and was increased very considerably.

From the middle of the 'fifties to the end of the 'seventies real wages undoubtedly increased considerably and reached again their former peak. At the end of the 'seventies real wages were again about as high as during the peak years of the 'thirties. Hours of work were lower. Child work did not play so great a rôle any more. On the other side labour conditions had worsened in many respects. While, during the first half of the century, a very considerable number of workers still had some kind of agricultural income the importance of this income had declined greatly up to the end of the 'seventies. During the 'sixties, and especially during the 'seventies, urbanization in Germany began to increase at a somewhat quicker pace than before. Many of the ill-effects of city congestion, especially of worsening housing conditions, began to take effect upon an increasing part of the German working class. And, of course, the intensity of work, the chief reason for the improvement in certain aspects of the worker's life, had increased very much.

During the 'eighties and 'nineties real wages continued to increase and reached a new peak at the end of the century. During these twenty years urbanization took full effect upon labour conditions. Housing conditions became as bad as in England, the agricultural resources of the industrial working class dried up almost completely. The shortening of working hours slowed up. And the intensity of work increased at a rapid pace.

At the same time, German capitalism began to invest heavily abroad. Foreign labour employed by German capital in Russia, in Turkey, in South America, in the Balkan countries, and in Austria-Hungary, subsequently in Africa too and in China, began to make extra profits for German capitalism.

These extra profits on the one side, and the increasing

pressure from organized labour on the other side, lead to a situation of the labour class which, perhaps might be called stabilized. During the 'eighties and the 'nineties labour conditions in general did probably not deteriorate in Germany just as in England the 'seventies and 'eighties probably were years of stabilization.

If in Germany, on the one hand, labour conditions suffered increasingly more from the growing effects of urbanization, while in England these ill-effects could barely be further increased at this time, in Germany, on the other hand, social insurance was introduced on a larger scale than in England.

On the whole one may assume that labour conditions in Germany did probably not deteriorate during the last decades of the nineteenth century.

But, just as in England the turn of the century meant a turn in the development of labour conditions, so also in Germany. Real wages remained about stable until the World War with a slight tendency to decline. Hours of work remained about stable with a slight tendency to be shortened. Urbanization and its ill-effects developed at a very rapid pace. Intensity of work increased quickly. More recently, the lost war, the double exploitation of German labour by the Allied as well as the German capitalists, led to a very rapid pauperization of German labour. Labour conditions in Germany deteriorated at a really unprecedented pace, and real wages during the last business-cycle reached the level of the seventies and the thirties of the last century.

Compared with the development in England, the degree of deterioration of labour conditions in post-War years was far worse in Germany. The double exploitation of German labour—by foreign and by home capitalists—has led back partly to some of the old forms of exploitation. The intensity of work has been increased immensely by means of far-reaching rationalization of production. At the same time there is a tendency, though not very obvious yet, to lengthen the working time again. In addition, real wages have been cut down to a level which makes it increasingly difficult for the German worker to keep up the intensity of work at the present level. The physical deterioration of the German worker has become very obvious during the last decade.

Without the still immensely rich resources of the English

capitalist, without vast sums of capital invested abroad at its disposal to employ foreign labour and to get high extra profits from this employment, the German capitalists took recourse again to some of the means of exploitation given up at the end of the 'fifties. The exploitation of labour in Germany began to take on again some of its more primitive forms.

And, just as England was master and example during the nineteenth century, it is not at all improbable that Germany becomes master and example for the twentieth century. A careful observer of the forms of exploitation in England may find also here the first signs of a return to some of the former methods of exploitation, discarded about ninety years ago. In the pace and methods of worsening labour conditions post-War Germany seems to precede other countries, which may follow very soon and very closely, and perhaps even surpass Germany.

If we compare the general development of labour conditions in Germany and England, we find definite similarities in the trend and its changes during the last 100 years and more. Only, in Germany the development always was more unfavourable to the worker than in England.

The decline of real wages, the general deterioration, and the increase of poverty and misery during the first half of the century were greater and lasted longer in Germany than in England. The subsequent increase in real wages and the improvement or stabilization of labour conditions in England were much more pronounced than the change in labour conditions in Germany. And during the twentieth century labour conditions deteriorated at a much quicker pace in Germany than in England.

While the movement of labour conditions in England was more favourable to the worker than that in Germany, the whole standard of living was higher too in England than in Germany. Therefore, a deterioration of labour conditions in Germany meant much more to the worker than the same percentage change in England.

The reason for this difference in the standard of labour conditions between Germany and England is that English

capitalism had much greater extra profits from employing
labour outside of the " mother country " than Germany, and
that English capitalism, through its earlier development and
larger spread, had a firmer grip on the world markets and a
securer position in world economics. Some traces of the
economic advantages of this position of English capitalism
could not but be found reflected also in the general conditions of the English working class.

.   .   .   .   .   .

The general average discussed above is composed of
several trends in individual industries. Quite generally, one
can observe that, as in England, so in Germany also real wages
in industry have increased more than real wages in agriculture. But during the 'seventies real wages in agriculture
increased considerably more than in industry. This impetus,
however, soon faded away, and agricultural labour conditions
again developed more unfavourably than those of industry
and transports.

Over the century as a whole the biggest increase of wages
probably occurred in the mining industry while the printing
industry lagged behind most. Printers, however, were
formerly considerably better paid than miners, and the
difference in the increase contributed rather to bring these
industries nearer to each other than to spread the difference
of their absolute standard of living.

Since the middle of the 'seventies wages probably increased
least in the transportation industry and most in chemicals.
Looking over the period as a whole wages in Germany were
more disparate 100 years ago than to-day, if we compare
averages for individual industries. And, while in former
times almost always some industries showed an absolute
improvement of labour conditions even if the general average
became worse and worse quite rapidly, during the twentieth
century it happened only rarely that an industry showed an
absolute improvement of labour conditions, and in post-War
times not one industry shows an improvement of labour
conditions.

.   .   .   .   .   .

For Germany more statistical material for the computation
of net real wages is available than for any other country.

Since it is quite impressive to see how wages change under
the influence of losses through unemployment and taxes, of
insurance benefits, etc., we give in the following table gross
wages, deductions from gross wages, and net real wages in
Germany.

FROM GROSS WAGES TO NET WAGES IN GERMANY
(1900 = 100)

Years	Gross Wages	Losses through Unemployment * %	Losses through Illness* %
1887–94	88	2.8	1.0
1894–1902	95	2.3	1.1
1903–9	110	2.1	1.3
1909–14	124	2.5	1.4
1924–35	181	15.0	1.9

Years	Taxes and Social Insurance Payments %	Trade Union Dues %	Net Money Wages	Net Real Wages
1887–94	3.3	—	88	92
1894–1902	4.0	—	95	97
1903–9	4.4	0.4	108	98
1909–14	5.0	0.8	121	96
1924–35	11.5	1.2	137	77

The table shows clearly the great, and what is more
important, the increasing effect of losses through unemployment, taxes, social insurance payments, upon the net wage
the worker takes home. Instead of being able to supplement
his wage by agricultural work, as was the case 100 years ago,
the worker to-day not only can add nothing to his wage
income, but has to suffer ever-increasing deductions.

. . . . . .

While absolute labour conditions developed even more
unfavourably for the worker in Germany than in England,
the abyss between the "two nations," at the same time,
widened much more in Germany than in England. The
rich in Germany became relatively much richer than the
rich in England, and the poor in Germany became relatively
much poorer than those in England. (See Table VI.)

While relative wages in England during the last post-War
cycle were barely half as low as about the middle of the

* Losses after social insurance benefits have been deducted.

century, relative wages in Germany equalled only one-fourth of them. The relative deterioration of the position of the working class in Germany was about twice as great as it was in England.

The terrible plight of the German worker can be seen very clearly from these three facts :

About the middle of the last century absolute labour conditions were worse in Germany than in England;

During the last post-War cycle absolute labour conditions in Germany as compared with those of the middle of the last century were worse than in England ;

At the same time, while absolute labour conditions in Germany deteriorated so much more than in England, relative labour conditions became worse in Germany at double the rate as in England.

Through this demarcation of the position of the German worker relative to the English worker, very much light is thrown on the position of the German worker, although not many studies of the actual living conditions of the German worker exist. It is permissible to draw a great number of conclusions from research studies pertaining to English labour conditions upon those of the German worker, if one simply pictures those of the German worker several shades darker.

Only about ten years separate the time when it becomes no longer possible for the ruling class to exploit the workers along the old accustomed lines, in England in the 'forties and in Germany in the 'fifties. And, up to this moment, there are only two more or less major differences in the development of labour conditions in the two countries : in England, the ill-effects of urbanization are more pronounced, while in Germany those of industrial patriarchalism and those of home work, are more in the foreground—and in Germany the deterioration of labour conditions grew more rapidly than in England.

There is almost no difference in the time when the ruling class again begins to decrease real wages as a means of increasing the rate of exploitation : it happens in both countries about the end of the nineteenth century. Both countries also are among the first to apply social insurance as a palliative against some of the effects of continuously increasing intensity of work upon the living conditions of the worker, though Germany started somewhat earlier. The fact that for some twenty years the increase in real wages did really somewhat improve labour conditions in England, even taking into account the very considerable increase in intensity of work, while a similar development cannot be observed in Germany is easily explained by the fact that English capitalism at that time made far more extra profits than German capitalism ever made—profits arising on the one side from the very extensive employment of cheap foreign labour, and on the other side from England's unique position as monopolist in many trades and commodities.

During the twentieth century the deterioration of labour conditions was perhaps not very different in both countries up to the World War. The very rapid deterioration of labour conditions in Germany during the post-War business-cycle is easily explained by the double pressure : exploitation by Allied and by German capitalists—under which the German worker had to work.

All these differences between England and Germany do not explain the fact that the relative position of the German worker became in the course of time so very much worse than that of the English worker. Of course, the rich in Germany are not richer than those in England ; on the contrary, the English ruling class is very much richer and mightier than the German ruling class. And as compared with the workers the German ruling class is by no means richer than that of England. But the difference between the condition of the working class and between that of the ruling class, though smaller in Germany than in England, has become in the course of time relatively very much greater in Germany than in England. The degree by which the abyss between these two classes has been widened was considerably greater in Germany than in England. I have not found any explanation for this development, but one can probably draw the conclusion from it, that the ruling class in Germany succeeded in exploiting the worker relatively much more than did the English ruling class.

TABLE I

Gross Money Wages in Germany

(1900 = 100)

Year	Industry and Transport	Total*	Year	Industry and Transport	Total*
1830–39	36	39	1870	65	64
			1871	67	66
1840–49	40	41	1872	75	73
			1873	84	81
1844	41	42	1874	86	85
1845	41	42	1875	85	86
1846	41	42	1876	79	82
1847	42	43	1877	75	80
1848	45	43	1878	74	79
1849	43	41	1879	71	77
1850	43	41	1880	71	78
1851	44	42	1881	72	78
1852	42	41	1882	75	80
1853	44	42	1883	75	80
1854	46	45	1884	76	81
1855	47	46	1885	77	81
1856	49	48	1886	77	81
1857	52	51	1887	79	82
1858	52	50	1888	82	84
1859	52	51	1889	85	88
1860	53	53	1890	87	90
1861	55	54	1891	87	91
186	55	55	1892	87	91
1863	55	55	1893	86	90
1864	56	56	1894	87	90
1865	56	56	1895	87	90
1866	58	58	1896	90	92
1867	59	59	1897	91	93
1868	61	61	1898	94	95
1869	63	62	1899	97	98

* Including agriculture.

TABLE I—*continued*

GROSS MONEY WAGES IN GERMANY

(1900 = 100)

Year	Industry and Transport	Total*	Year	Industry and Transport	Total*
1900	100	100	1924	135	132
1901	99	99	1925	169	166
1902	99	100	1926	182	176
1903	100	101	1927	190	187
1904	103	103	1928	205	200
1905	106	106	1929	215	210
1906	112	111			
1907	118	115	1930	218	213
1908	117	115	1931	206	203
1909	118	117	1932	177	175
			1933	170	170
1910	121	119	1934	170	168
1911	124	122	1935	170	168
1912	128	126			
1913	133	131			
1914	134	132			

TABLE II

GROSS MONEY WAGES BY INDUSTRIES IN GERMANY

(1900 = 100)

Trade			1825	1833	1844	1855	1865	1875
Building	..	..	..	—	—	40	48	53	79
Metals	,.	..	..	30	31	47	46	58	85
Textiles	..	..	..	—	—	—	49	54	82
Wood	..	..	..	—	—	—	—	44	95
Printing	..	..	..	—	52	53	58	70	92
Transportation	..	..	..	—	—	—	—	—	99
Mining	..	..	..	27	29	31	42	63	83
Average	..	..	..	—	—	41	47	56	85

Trade			1885	1895	1905	1913	1924	1934
Building	..	..	..	74	87	110	139	134	163
Metals	..	..	..	81	89	102	123	124	148
Textiles	..	..	..	86	93	108	124	127	170
Wood	..	..	..	71	88	110	138	137	195
Printing	..	..	..	88	97	109	129	130	184
Chemicals	..	..	..	73	91	103	146	147	202
Transportation	..	..	..	83	89	108	141	149	195
Mining	..	..	..	73	77	99	125	135	164
Average	..	..	..	77	87	106	133	135	170

* Including agriculture.

TABLE III
COST OF LIVING, GERMANY

Year	Index	Year	Index	Year	Index
1820	49	1860	74	1900	100
1821	43	1861	77	1901	101
1822	44	1862	78	1902	102
1823	45	1863	72	1903	102
1824	36	1864	68	1904	103
1825	35	1865	71	1905	107
1826	39	1866	75	1906	113
1827	46	1867	88	1907	114
1828	47	1868	89	1908	114
1829	48	1869	82	1909	117
1830	50	1870	83	1910	120
1831	57	1871	90	1911	124
1832	54	1872	94	1912	130
1833	52	1873	104	1913	130
1834	45	1874	108	1914*	130
1835	46	1875	99		
1836	45	1876	99		
1837	46	1877	100		
1838	52	1878	95		
1839	54	1879	93	1924	166
				1925	182
1840	53	1880	99	1926	184
1841	52	1881	100	1927	192
1842	55	1882	98	1928	197
1843	58	1883	98	1929	200
1844	53	1884	93	1930	193
1845	57	1885	91	1931	177
1846	68	1886	89	1932	157
1847	79	1887	89	1933	153
1848	57	1888	91	1934	157
1849	50	1889	95	1935	160
1850	49	1890	98		
1851	55	1891	100		
1852	64	1892	99		
1853	69	1893	97		
1854	81	1894	96		
1855	87	1895	95		
1856	85	1896	94		
1857	72	1897	96		
1858	69	1898	99		
1859	69	1899	99		

* First half of the year.

TABLE IV

Gross Real Wages in Germany

(Total of Industry, Transport and Agriculture, weighted according
to number of employed and amount of wages paid per worker.)

Year	Index	Year	Index	Year	Index
1830–39	78	1870	77	1900	100
		1871	73	1901	98
1840–49	71	1872	78	1902	98
		1873	78	1903	99
1844	80	1874	79	1904	100
1845	74	1875	87	1905	99
1846	62	1876	83	1906	98
1847	54	1877	80	1907	101
1848	74	1878	83	1908	101
1849	81	1879	83	1909	100
1850	83	1880	79	1910	99
1851	76	1881	78	1911	99
1852	64	1882	82	1912	97
1853	61	1883	82	1913	101
1854	55	1884	87	1914	102
1855	53	1885	89		
1856	56	1886	91	1924	80
1857	71	1887	92	1925	91
1858	73	1888	93	1926	96
1859	74	1889	93	1927	97
				1928	101
1860	72	1890	92	1929	105
1861	70	1891	91		
1862	71	1892	92	1930	111
1863	76	1893	93	1931	115
1864	82	1894	94	1932	112
1865	79	1895	95	1933	111
1866	77	1896	98	1934	107
1867	67	1897	97	1935	105
1868	69	1898	96		
1869	76	1899	99		

TABLE V

NET REAL WAGES, IN GERMANY*

(Cyclical Averages, 1900 = 100)

Cycle	Index
1830–9†	78
1840–9†	71
1844–52	72
1852–9	63
1860–7	74
1868–78	78
1879–86	84
1887–94	92
1894–1902	97
1903–9	98
1909–14	96
1924–35	77

SOURCES AND REMARKS

Wages of non-Agricultural Workers, 1830 to 1914. Computed on the basis of material collected and published in Jürgen Kuczynski *Wages in Germany, 1820 to 1935*, U.S. Bureau of Labor Statistics.

Wages of Agricultural Workers, 1830 to 1914. Computed and estimated on the basis of data contained in the following studies : Anna Neumann, *Die Bewegung der Löhne der ländlichen ' freien ' Arbeiter im Königreich Preussen vom Ausgang des 18. Jahrhunderts bis 1850*; v.d., Goltz, *Die Lage der ländlichen Arbeiter im Deutschen Reich*; Meitzen, *Der Boden und die landwirtschaftlichen Verhältnisse des Preussischen Staates*; Udo Eggert, *Die Bewegung der Holzpreise und Tagelohnsätze in den preussischen Staatsforsten von 1800 bis 1879* (Zeitschrift des Kgl. Preussischen Statistischen Bureaus, 1883); Schütze, *Studien über die Entwicklung der Lohnverhältnisse ländlicher Arbeiter in Norddeutschland seit 1870*; Asmis, *Zur Entwicklung der Landarbeiterlöhne in Preussen* (Landwirtschaftl. Jahrbücher, 1919); Klatt, *Geschichtliche Entwicklung der Landarbeiterverhältnisse in Ostpreussen*; Hucho, *Die Naturalentlohnung in der deutschen Landwirtschaft*; *Festschrift zur 50 jährigen Jubelfeier des Provinziallandwirtschaftlichen Vereins zu Bremervörde*; Frege, *Zur Lohnbewegung der letzten 100 Jahre*.

* 1830–87 gross real wages per full-time week, 1887–1935 taking into account wage losses through unemployment and illness, taxes and insurance payments, and income gains through insurance benefits, 1903–35 taking into account trade union dues.

† 1830–9 and 1840–9 decennial and not cyclical averages.

Wages, 1924 *to* 1935. Wages for manufacturing industry, mining, transportation and building, computed on the basis of the official data published by the Statistische Reichsamt. As to the methods of computation, cf. *Die Lage des deutschen Industrie-Arbeiters*, by Jürgen and Marguerite Kuczynski, and the monthly wage survey in the *Finanzpolitische Korrespondenz*, Jahrgang, 1929–33. Wages of agricultural workers were computed on the basis of the yearly survey in the *Statistische Jahrbuch für das Deutsche Reich*, and in the *Landarbeiter-Archiv*, and of the study by Helmerking, *Untersuchungen über die vergleichsweise Höhe der Landarbeiterlöhne in Deutschland vor und nach dem Kriege.*

Unemployment. 1887–1903 estimates ; 1903–14 and 1924–32 trade union statistics ; 1933, 1934 and 1935 estimates. Cf. Jürgen Kuczynski, *Die Entwicklung der Lage der Arbeiterschaft in Europa und Amerika*, 1870–1933 ; in this study, through a printing mistake, unemployment for 1896 is given as 0.1 per cent instead of 0.6 per cent.

Illness. The percentage of time lost through illness is computed from the official statistics of days lost through illness per member of the health insurance scheme, as published in the *Statistische Jahrbuch für das Deutsche Reich.*

Taxes and Social Insurance Payments. Estimates for 1914 and 1924–33, cf. *Finanzpolitische Korrespondenz*, 1929–33.

Social Insurance Benefits. Cf. the above-mentioned studies ; the benefits from health insurance are estimated on the basis of the official rate.

Cost of Living, 1820–1914. For food prices cf. Jürgen Kuczynski, *Wages in Germany*, 1820–1935, U.S. Bureau of Labor Statistics. Rents for 1820 to 1890 are computed or estimated on the basis of data for the following years and towns : 1820–50 Berlin, 1850–70 Berlin and Halle, 1870–80 Berlin, Halle, Hamburg and Leipzig, 1880 same cities and Breslau and Dresden, 1885 same cities as 1880 and Magdeburg, and 1890 same cities as 1885 without Dresden. For statistical sources see those given below for 1890–1914. Rents 1890–1914 computed or estimated on the basis of data for the following cities : Barmen, Berlin, Breslau, Chemnitz, Halle, Hamburg, Jena, Leipzig, Luebeck, Magdeburg, Strassburg and Stuttgart. For most of these cities rent data were not available for a series of consecutive years, but only at intervals which differed from city to city. Statistical sources for rent data for the years 1820–1914 are : *Kosten der Lebenshaltung in Deutschen Grosstbdten* (published by the Verein für Sozialpolitik) ; *Zeitschrift des Kgl. Preussischen Statistischen Bureaus*, 1872 ; Hampke, *Das Ausgabebudget der Privatwirtschaften* ; Verein fur Sozialpolitik, *Neue Untersuchungen ueber die Wohnungsfrage in Deutschland und im Ausland* ; Verein fuer Sozialpolitik, *Die Wohnungsnot der armeren Klassen in deutschen Gorsstaedten* ; Duncker and Rutenberg, two articles in the *Monatsschrift fuer Deutsches Staedte– und Gemeindewesen*, 1857 ; *Monatsberichte des Statistischen Amts der Stadt Chemnitz*, 1928 ; Walter Voigt, *Die*

H

Loehne in den Stiftungsbetrieben von Carl Zeiss und Schott & Gen. The index of rents was weighted 1, the index of food was weighted 3.

Cost of Living, 1914 *and* 1924–35. We used the official cost-of-living index published in the *Statistische Jahrbuch für das Deutsche Reich.*

The data on wages in Germany are considerably inferior to the collection made by Bowley and Wood for England. The collection for Germany made by myself does not contain as many data as that of Bowley and Wood, and the data are even more incongruous than those collected by Bowley and Wood because they are not only a mixture of trade union rates, general rates, and actual wages paid, but in addition they contain also average weekly wages actually paid, thus including wage losses through short-time, and average yearly wages. For pre-War years the whole food industry and the clothing industry are not represented at all. For many industries wage data are available only since the 'forties or 'fifties or even later. Occasionally daily wages are used instead of weekly wages. Especially bad are the data for agricultural wages, which are taken from a number of sources the reliability of which cannot be checked ; many interpolations had to be made to arrive at an index. The different industrial areas of Germany are not covered sufficiently and the wages of this or that region, in this or that branch of an industry very often received too high a weight compared with the number employed. City wages are preponderant in much too high a degree. Although the collection of wages is a very insufficient one, it is by far the best available, and the only one aiming to some extent at comprehensiveness.

Even worse than the wage index is the cost-of-living index. For pre-War years it only pertains to food prices and to rents. And the index of rents though probably better than that for England, cannot be called more than a very rough estimate.

Since many of the other factors taken into account for the computation of net real wages are based on estimates, it is obvious that our figures are at best approximations. The scepticism expressed in regard to the statistics for England applies even more to the wage statistics for Germany. The trend of wages is shown roughly for England as well as for Germany—but the year-to-year data should be regarded more as indefinite shades of the line along which wages moved than as the actual line itself.

TABLE VI

RELATIVE WAGES IN GERMANY

(1900 = 100)

Cycles	Physical Volume of Industrial and Agricultural per capita Production	Wholesale Prices	Retail Prices
1860–7	53	93	75
1868–78	62	100	95
1879–86	70	80	95
1887–94	82	79	96
1894–1902	102	79	98
1903–9	121	89	110
1909–14	127	97	125
1924–35	115	114	177

Cycles	Industrial and Agricultural per capita Production, corrected according to relative Price Movements	Real Wages	Relative Wages
1860–7	44	74	170
1868–78	59	78	133
1879–86	83	84	101
1887–94	99	92	93
1894–1902	127	97	76
1903–9	150	98	65
1909–14	164	96	58
1924–35	178	77	44

Industrial Production. Cf. Rolf Wagenführ, *Die Industriewirtschaft, Entwicklungstendenzen der deutschen und der internationalen Industrie-produktion,* 1860–1932, and the current data given in the *Vierteljahrshefte zur Konjunkturforschung,* published by the Institut für Konjunkturforschung, Berlin.

Agricultural Production. Data for 1860–1924 used for this index pertain solely to crop production, and are taken from the official crop statistics, from Hans Wolfram Graf Finck von Finckenstein : *Die Getreidewirtschaft Preussens von* 1800 *bis* 1930, and from the official cultivation statistics. For the years 1924 to 1935 we used the current estimates made by the Institut für Konjunkturforschung.

Total Production. Agricultural and industrial production are weighted according to the value estimates by the Institut für

Konjunkturforschung in Konjunkturstatistisches Handbuch, 1933.

Wholesale Prices. Cf. Alfred Jacobs and Hans Richter, *Die Grosshandelspreise in Deutschland von* 1792 *bis* 1934, and the official wholesale price index for 1934 and 1935.

Population. We used the official population statistics.

Cost of Living. See p. 97 of this book.

Real Wages. See pp. 96–97 of this book.

It is obvious that our computations are only rough approximations. The wage index is worse than that for England. On the other hand, the production index is better because it includes agricultural production. The cost-of-living index is probably better than that for England, while the wholesale price index is probably worse.

From the errors certainly contained in our index it is not possible to conclude that the relative wage index has a bias in this or that direction. We incline to the opinion that there is no definite bias at all.

CHAPTER IV

LABOUR CONDITIONS IN FRANCE

IN looking over the development of real wages in England and Germany, we found a striking similarity between the wage trend in both countries. It is therefore not so astonishing to find the same pattern in France too.

As in England and Germany, labour conditions deteriorated in France during the first half of the nineteenth century, especially through a decline of real wages. Our table of business-cycle averages of net real wages, does not contain any averages for the years prior to 1852. But even the haphazardly chosen figures for 1820, 1830, 1840 and 1850, the only years for which wage data are available in a sufficient number to warrant the risk of computing average wages in industry and agriculture, show that real wages have at least not increased. If we take into consideration that our wage data do not give the proper weight to the increasing number of women and children employed, that they do not take into account the increasing burden of unemployment in the 'forties, then it must seem obvious, even from our table, that real wages up to the end of the 'fifties declined quite considerably. As in England and in Germany, modern capitalism started intensive exploitation of the workers first by extending the working-day and by decreasing real wages. These methods as chief means of exploitation were applied in England only until the end of the 'forties, while in France, as in Germany, extensive use of these methods was resorted to until far into the 'fifties.

Summarizing the development of labour conditions from the beginning of the post-Napoleonic era until the end of the reign of Louis Philippe, Levasseur writes—and we must remember that Levasseur believed in the progress of the labouring class and in an improvement of labour conditions under a capitalist régime :*

* Emile Levasseur, *Histoire des classes ovrières et de l'industrie en France de* 1789 *à* 1870, II, p. 823.

" The labour class was divided more and more into three groups : the workers in the small establishments whose material conditions had not changed appreciably since the ' Restauration ' ; the workers in the big industrial establishments who increased in numbers and whose wages often were smaller and whose living conditions were worse than under the ' Restauration ' ; and finally the workers in the textile home industry whose living and labour conditions were made miserable through industrial competition."

It is the same in France as in England and in Germany : all authorities agree that labour conditions during the first half of the century deteriorated.

At the end of the 'fifties a change in the policy of the capitalist class occurred in France as it occurred in Germany, and as it had already taken place ten years before in England : labour conditions had become so unbearable, the physique of the workers had suffered so much that it became impossible to continue production at the same rate and to keep up the intensity of work—to say nothing of a further increase of productivity—without a considerable improvement in the nutrition of the worker and a decided shortening of the working-day.

Consequently, in the following business-cycle real wages began to increase considerably and reached at least the level of the 'twenties. In the course of the next ten years, after the war with Germany had been lost, real wages did not increase ; they probably remained stable. The impetus of improving a considerable number of aspects of the condition of French labour was thus a short-lived one, and at the end of the 'seventies real wages were approximately as high as about sixty years ago, in the beginning of the 'twenties.

The rise of real wages from the 'fifties to the 'sixties was accompanied, of course, by an increase in the intensity of work. Labour conditions were improved in many respects not to please labour, but in order to enable employers to increase the intensity of work, in order to increase the rate of exploitation, the rate of surplus value. Reviewing the period from 1850 to 1870 Levasseur writes :*

" The number of workers increased and they filled the factories more and more ; many of them lived a miserable

* l.c., p. 834.

existence and had to suffer privation if unemployed. But one cannot say that the living conditions of the workers had deteriorated generally. The increase of nominal wages and probably also of real wages towards the end of the ' Empire,' the increase in the amount of food consumed and in the savings accounts indicate the contrary."

The argument that increasing real wages and increasing food consumption necessarily mean an improvement in labour conditions is not convincing. A simultaneous great increase in the intensity of work and the accumulated ill-effect of city congestion, may very well compensate or more than compensate the increase in real wages and the accompanying increase in the consumption of food.

But perhaps labour conditions, all aspects being taken into account, did not deteriorate during the 'sixties and remained more or less stable. It might even be possible that labour conditions improved a little, though that is not very probable. For, during the 'sixties, French capital began the employment and exploitation of foreign labour, that is of workers outside of France, at an unprecedented rate. C. K. Hobson, the greatest authority on foreign investments* thinks that the activity of French capital in foreign countries approximately equalled that of the English during the 'sixties. And it is not astounding that some of the enormous extra profits derived from the employment of labour outside of France have been applied to (not for) the benefit of French labour by French capitalism, be it to insure an uninterrupted production process without strikes and labour struggles as far as that is possible, or be it for other similar reasons.

During the 'seventies, our index of real wages shows almost no change. It is very probable that during these years labour conditions deteriorated at a comparatively quick rate under the influence of double exploitation, directly through French capitalists, and indirectly through the capitalists of other countries, who lent France the money to pay the war tributes levied by Germany in 1871.

During the 'eighties and 'nineties, and during the first years of the present century, real wages increased. But this increase did not signify an improvement of labour conditions. Not only did the intensity of work increase—but, and this

* Cf., C. K. Hobson, *The Export of Capital.*

is in many respects of the greatest importance : the close connection between the city worker and the country, which often supplied part of the family income, was dissolved more and more. While in former times industrial wages often were supplemented either by gardening by the industrial workers or by food sent from the country, where part of the family lived, these supplements began to cease during the last twenty years of the nineteenth century. There are many other ill-effects, such as those arising from increasing city congestion, etc., which contributed to cancel and over-compensate the effect of increasing real wages on the worker's standard of living. On the whole, it is very probable that the living conditions of the working class in France deteriorated slightly during the third of a century preceding the World War.

After the World War labour conditions undoubtedly became worse, real wages decreased, intensity of work increased immensely—especially owing to the reconstruction and rationalization process applied to French industry with the means of extra profits derived from exploiting the German worker.

Looking over the development of labour conditions in France during the whole of the nineteenth and twentieth centuries, and comparing this development with that in Germany and England, one is probably right in summarizing :

Absolute labour conditions of the French worker were probably never quite so bad as those of the English or the German worker. The intensity of work was always lower than in England or Germany. This as well as the close connection between country and city, and the fact that even after this connection became almost dissolved as far as the big cities are concerned, a great many workers still lived in the country or were agricultural workers, all this prevented the development from reaching such depths of human misery as we found it and find it in England and Germany.

As to the development of labour conditions, undoubtedly the German worker is worst off as compared with 100 years ago—owing especially to the very great deterioration of labour conditions in post-War years. The English worker is best off (always relatively, as compared with a century ago), because of the long period of gigantic accumulation of extra profits from the employment of foreign labour by English capital outside of England. For almost fifty years labour conditions in England proper (very probably) improved or remained more or less stable. In between the German worker and the English worker stands the French worker : absolutely better off than the two others considering all the factors determining labour conditions, but in relation to the situation of 100 years ago, worse off than the English worker and better off than the German worker.

As to the relative position of the French worker (relative to other groups within French economic society) no data sufficient for computing relative wages are available, and therefore it is impossible to measure with any degree, not of accuracy but at least of approximation, the relative deterioration of the position of the French working class—but it cannot be doubted that such a deterioration has taken place.

TABLE I

WAGES IN FRANCE

Non-Agricultural Workers.   (1895 = 100)

Year	Gross Money Wages	Net Money Wages	Cost of Living	Gross Real Wages	Net Real Wages
1820	46	—	74	62	—
1830	48	—	77	62	—
1840	51	—	79	65	—
1850	54	—	79	68	—
1851	53	—	78	68	—
1852	53	—	80	66	—
1853	55	—	91	60	—
1854	59	—	103	57	—
1855	60	—	111	54	—
1856	59	—	113	52	—
1857	62	—	104	60	—
1858	64	—	93	69	—
1859	65	—	87	75	—
1860	66	—	99	67	—
1861	70	—	105	67	—
1862	71	—	101	70	—

TABLE I—*continued*

Year	Gross Money Wages	Net Money Wages	Cost of Living	Gross Real Wages	Net Real Wages
1863	72	—	99	73	—
1864	72	—	95	76	—
1865	72	—	93	77	—
1866	74	—	98	76	—
1867	75	—	106	71	—
1868	77	—	108	71	—
1869	78	—	100	78	—
1870	79	—	102	77	—
1871	79	—	122	65	—
1872	82	—	111	74	—
1873	83	—	116	72	—
1874	84	—	119	71	—
1875	86	—	102	84	—
1876	86	—	106	81	—
1877	86	—	109	79	—
1878	88	—	112	79	—
1879	89	—	110	81	—
1880	93	—	115	81	—
1881	96	—	115	83	—
1882	98	—	112	88	—
1883	99	—	113	88	—
1884	99	—	110	90	—
1885	98	—	106	92	—
1886	98	—	106	92	—
1887	98	—	105	93	—
1888	98	—	99	99	—
1889	99	—	101	98	—
1890	99	—	104	95	—
1891	99	—	106	93	—
1892	100	—	100	100	—
1893	100	—	98	102	—
1894	100	—	101	99	—
1895	100	100	100	100	100
1896	101	101	99	102	102
1897	102	102	99	103	103
1898	104	104	100	104	104
1899	107	107	98	109	109
1900	108	108	99	109	109
1901	107	106	93	115	114
1902	105	102	91	115	112
1903	107	105	99	108	106
1904	107	104	97	110	107

TABLE I—*continued*

Year	Gross Money Wages	Net Money Wages	Cost of Living	Gross Real Wages	Net Real Wages
1905	107	105	93	115	113
1906	112	111	92	122	121
1907	113	112	97	116	115
1908	117	114	99	118	115
1909	118	118	98	120	120
1910	120	121	102	118	119
1911	122	123	111	110	111
1912	123	124	115	107	108
1913	124	126	112	111	112
1914	123	124	110	112	113
1922	482	492	396	122	124
1923	529	550	470	112	117
1924	588	610	536	110	114
1925	625	648	570	110	114
1926	738	766	669	110	114
1927	740	715	697	107	103
1928	777	793	722	108	110
1929	865	898	825	105	109
1930	932	968	851	110	114
1931	930	868	852	109	102
1932	899	737	828	109	89
1933	870	711	792	110	90
1934	865	689	787	110	88
1935	840	625	750	112	83

TABLE II

GROSS MONEY WAGES BY INDIVIDUAL INDUSTRIES
(1892 = 100)

Trade		1850	1855	1860	1865	1870	1875	1880
Building	.. ..	54	58	61	69	72	75	96
Mining	.. ..	50	55	59	63	72	84	83
Textiles	.. ..	47	55	65	66	77	87	92
Metals	..	—	—	—	—	86	93	95
Woodworking	..	—	—	—	—	80	84	93
Printing	.. ..	—	—	—	—	88	92	100
Sugar industry	..	—	—	—	—	—.	—	—
Tobacco industry	..	—	—	—	—	—	—	—

TABLE II—*continued*

Trade	1885	1892	1896	1901	1906	1911
Building	100	100	100	102	—	129
Mining	88	100	97	114	112	121
Textiles	102	100	102	102	105	107
Metals	97	100	102	109	116	125
Woodworking	97	100	100	107	—	—
Printing	100	100	100	104	—	—
Sugar industry	105	100	100	108	110	119
Tobacco industry	—	100	105	112	123	135

TABLE III

NET REAL WAGES IN FRANCE*

(Cyclical Averages, 1895 = 100)

Cycle	Index
1820	79
1830	79
1840	78
1850	79
1852–8	68
1859–68	82
1868–78	83
1879–86	90
1887–95	98
1895–1903	107
1903–8	114
1909–14	114
1922–35	105

SOURCES AND REMARKS

Wages, 1820 *to* 1850. Cf. *Salaires et coût de l'existence à diverses époques jusqu'en*, 1910, *Statistique générale de la France*, Paris, 1911.

Wages, 1850 *to* 1914. A combination of wages in the mining, sugar, and tobacco industry (cf. *Annuaire Statistique*, 1933), metal, printing, building, and woodworking industry (cf. R. Kuczynski, *Arbeitslohn und Arbeitszeit in Europa und Amerika*, 1870–1909), textile (men), building (Paris), and metal industry (Simiand, *Le Salaire*). In most cases the original sources give daily wage data. For metals and building the data given by Kuczynski and Simiand were combined. The individual industrial series were weighted according to the number employed per industry.

Wages, 1922 *to* 1935. " Salaires de certaines categories d'ouvriers dans les chefs-lieux de departement et les villes où siègent les Conseils de prud'hommes," *Bulletin de la Statistique générale de la France*, for 1924–35. For 1922 to 1924 wages pertaining to mining, sugar, and tobacco industry only; source cf. above.

* Industrial and agricultural workers.

Wages of Agricultural Workers, 1820 *to* 1935. We combined the data given by Simiand for France, Paris excluded, Vol. III, first table.

Cost of Living, 1820 *to* 1887. Cf. " Salaires et coût de l'existence." Paris, 1911. The data pertain to food, heating, light, and rent. As far as data on rents were not available for consecutive years, they were interpolated by assuming that rents had moved with an equal yearly velocity between the two years for which the data are available.

Cost of Living, 1887 *to* 1911. Cf. J. Kuczynski, *Die Entwicklung der Lage der Arbeiterschaft in Europa und Amerika,* 1870–1933.

Cost of Living, 1911 *to* 1914. For 1911, 1913 and 1914, cf. *Bulletin de la Statistique générale,* 1918, p. 240. Figure for 1912 estimated.

Cost of Living, 1922 *to* 1935. For 1922 to 1924 we used the data for a family of four, and for 1924 to 1935 those for " Prix Mensuel de Pension," given in the *Bulletin de la Statistique générale de la France,* and pertaining to food and rent.

Unemployment, 1895 *to* 1914. Cf. *Annuaire Statistique.* Unemployment for 1914 estimated.

Unemployment, 1922 *to* 1935. Cf. J. Kuczynski, *Die Entwicklung der Lage der Arbeiterschaft in Europa und Amerika,* 1870–1933 ; unemployment for 1934 was estimated at 17 per cent and short-time computed into unemployment at 8 per cent ; for 1935 the corresponding figures are 20 and 10 per cent.

The wage data for France are even worse than those for Germany. As a whole they cover a much smaller number of workers, they are mostly data on actual wages, pertaining mostly to the working-day instead of to the working-week. On the other hand, they cover a greater number of workers in the consumption industries than the data for England or Germany. The data for agricultural workers are slightly better than those for Germany, but much worse than those for England. They are available only for a small number of years scattered over the whole of the 115 years under review.

The cost-of-living data are considerably better than those for England and Germany as far as the nineteenth century and the pre-War period of the twentieth century are concerned. For post-War years probably no great industrial country has such utterly inadequate and so many differing cost-of-living data as France.

But the trend of wages in general is so evident that though the year-to-year data are for some years probably utterly insufficient while for others quite adequate, the business-cycle averages are good enough to serve as indicators of the trend of real wages.

LABOUR CONDITIONS
IN WESTERN EUROPE

It is only possible to write this chapter under this heading because labour conditions changed so very similarly in England, Germany, and France.

There are only two other small industrial countries whose labour conditions we have not investigated : Belgium and Luxembourg. Spain is mainly agricultural, the same holds true, for most of the time under review, of Holland ; and the number of agricultural wage earners in these two countries is small.

In Belgium, labour conditions as far as we can find out from the data available, moved very similar to those in France and the same holds true of labour conditions in Luxembourg.

But even if labour conditions in Luxembourg and Belgium had developed differently, the number of workers in England, Germany and France is so great as compared with that of these two countries, that a different development of wages in these two countries, and also in Spain and Holland would not have affected considerably the movement of average labour conditions in the whole of Western Europe.

Since Western Europe is the cradle of modern industrial capitalism, the survey of wages and labour conditions in Western Europe is at the same time a review of the history of labour conditions in the beginning of industrial capitalism.

Common to all three countries in the beginning of the spread of industrial capitalism over a preponderantly agricultural and commercial area is a period during which the physical deterioration of the working class increases quickly and spreads rapidly.

Long hours of work, increasingly long hours per day, low wages, increasingly deficient purchasing power undermine the health and the working capacity of the working class.

Since the aim of capitalist society is the appropriation of surplus value by the capitalists, and since this appropriation

110

found at the end of this period its natural limit in the physical " deficiencies " of the human body which " unfortunately " needs a certain minimum amount of food and rest, capitalist society had to change its methods of appropriation of surplus value.

This change of methods brought for the workers better food and fewer hours of work. It meant at the same time increasing intensity of work per hour. The body of the worker was not spared during this period, which stretches from the 'fifties to the end of the last century. It only was handled more carefully in order to be able to do a much more strenuous job : producing goods at a rate and at an intensity unforeseen in the previous period.

During this second period extensive exploitation of foreign labour, of labour outside of Western Europe was added to the activities of Western capitalism. In consequence of this enormous broadening of the field of exploitation gigantic extra profits were made. These gigantic extra profits allowed the ruling class in Western Europe the luxury of giving for a short period some of the extra profits to the workers at home, chiefly in order to ensure industrial peace which was threatened more and more through better organization and more militant tactics of labour. Another reason for letting the workers share a little in these extra profits was to get the help of the workers in the finishing struggle with the landed interests.

In consequence of this temporary sharing of the workers in the extra profits, made from the exploitation of workers employed abroad, labour conditions during the second half of the nineteenth century partly improved absolutely or remained stable, that is, they at least ceased to deteriorate in the " mother countries." This improvement or stabilization of labour conditions in England, Germany and France, during the second half of the nineteenth century must, however, not cloud the issue. Western capitalism continued also in the second half of the nineteenth century to increase the exploitation of labour, and if we would be able to compute average wages and an index of average labour conditions of all labour employed by English, or French, or German capitalism, whether this labour be employed abroad or at home, then we would see that labour conditions of all workers combined, those employed at home and abroad, continued to deteriorate also during the second half of the nineteenth century, and probably deteriorated more quickly than during the first half of the nineteenth century.

During the twentieth century, when the rate of extra profits (but not the mass of extra profits) began to decline, labour conditions deteriorated also in the home countries, real wages declined, even taking into account the benefits from social insurance, and misery and pauperism in England, Germany and France were on the increase again.

To-day, labour conditions in England, in Germany, and in France, are undoubtedly and considerably worse than they were forty years ago. The purchasing power of the worker is smaller and the intensity of work is very much higher.

A process has set in, very similar to that in the beginning of the history of industrial capitalism. The worker is less and less able physically to stand the pace of production, to keep up the intensity of work.

But while about eighty years ago capitalism was able to change its methods of exploitation because of increasing extra profits from labour employed abroad, the situation to-day is quite different. The exploitation of labour abroad is still growing in intensity and extension—but the world market begins to shrink relatively, new markets are not being opened up, the realization of profits is becoming more and more difficult.

A world in which imperialism, in which industrial monopolism predominates, a world of which one-sixth is closed to exploitation by Western capitalism through the erection of a workers' republic, a world shaken again and again by economic crises and wars, a world in which labour increases in strength through better organization and better strategy makes it impossible for Western capitalism to return to the former methods of increasing the exploitation of labour.

As far as the future of labour conditions under Western capitalism is concerned, one can only expect a further decline of the purchasing power of the worker and probably a slow lengthening of the hours of work per day while at the same time unemployment and short-time will show a tendency to grow. As long as Western capitalism still holds the sceptre a rapid deterioration of labour conditions is to be expected.

INDEX